MONEY SKILLS FOR TEENS

A Beginner's Guide to Budgeting,
Saving, and Investing

*Everything a Teenager Should Know
About Personal Finance*

FERNE BOWE

Money Skills for Teens. A Beginner's Guide to Budgeting, Saving, and Investing. Everything a Teenager Should Know About Personal Finance

ISBN: 978-1-915833-09-9

JOIN OUR
ADVANCE READER
GROUP

and get FREE advance access to all our latest books!

To join our exclusive group:

SCAN
HERE

TABLE OF CONTENTS

7   **Introduction**
9   **How to Use this Book**

11   **PART ONE: Understanding Money—The Basics**
11   **Chapter 1.** Money (Really) Matters
18   **Chapter 2.** Banking 101
28   **Chapter 3.** Credit Reports—Why Your Credit Score Matters!
39   **Chapter 4.** Jobs & Money
49   **Chapter 5.** Keeping It Private—Frauds and Scams

57   **PART TWO: Budgeting and Savvy Spending**
57   **Chapter 6.** Budgeting—Making a Plan (and Sticking to It)
68   **Chapter 7.** Spending—How to Get More for Less!

79   **PART THREE: Borrowing, Debt, and Big-Ticket Item Purchases**
79   **Chapter 8.** Introduction to Borrowing Money and Debt
94   **Chapter 9.** Big-Ticket Item Purchases
98   **Chapter 10.** An Introduction to Car Ownership
102   **Chapter 11.** An Introduction to Home Ownership

107   **PART FOUR: Your Way to Wealth**
107   **Chapter 12.** Saving—Your Rainy Day Fund
118   **Chapter 13.** Investing—Building Wealth

139   **PART FIVE: The Future of Money**
140   **Chapter 14.** From Cash to Cashless

147   **Let's get started!!!**

INTRODUCTION

Congratulations! You're a teen, and the world is yours for the taking!

It's an exciting time, but it can also be daunting. With so much to learn and so many new experiences, it's easy to feel overwhelmed. But that's ok. It's perfectly normal to feel overwhelmed by the responsibility of growing up.

That's where this book comes in. To help you with one of the biggest responsibilities and challenges every young adult has to face: Money.

This book is here to help you understand the concept of money, what it is, how to earn and save it—and how to spend it wisely.

We'll cover all the basics, like how to open bank accounts, avoid scams, understand credit scores, budget wisely, and avoid debt. And we'll dig into more complex topics like how to get a mortgage, lease a car, and invest in the stock market.

We'll explain the facts and use real-life examples that make money matters easy to understand. Throughout the pages, you'll find valuable tips and tricks, interesting stats, and even some fun activities to put your knowledge into practice.

By the end of this book, you'll have all the financial knowledge you need to feel confident in navigating the world of money. Including:

- How to select and open a bank account
- An understanding of credit cards and how to establish a good credit score
- How to create a budgeting plan
- How to develop money-saving habits
- How to start investing in the stock market

And much more!

This book is designed to be your go-to guide for your financial journey into adulthood. To give you the solid foundations of money skills, knowledge, and experiences to help you make wise financial decisions throughout your life.

HOW TO USE THIS BOOK

This book is divided into five parts:

- Understanding Money

- Budgeting & Savvy Spending

- Borrowing, Debt, and Big Ticket Item Purchases

- Your Way to Wealth

- The Future of Money

Going through each, one by one will give you a good understanding of the world of money. You'll start with the basics and build your knowledge as you progress through the book. Feel free to jump around if there's something specific that interests you or if there's something you want to learn more about.

Finally, this book is intended to be the start of your financial journey. We'll point you in the right direction, but it's up to you to take action and make it happen. That means using what you learn, putting it into practice, and continuing to read and learn more about money and how it works. Remember, the more you know, the better decisions you will make!

Ready? Let's go!

PART ONE

UNDERSTANDING MONEY – THE BASICS

CHAPTER 1. MONEY (REALLY) MATTERS

Money makes the world go round.
Money talks.
Money doesn't grow on trees.
Money can't buy you happiness.

These are just some of the many sayings you may have heard about money. Some love it, some hate it, yet most of us don't know much about it.

Whether we like it or not, money is a massive part of our lives. It's how we get by day to day; it's a tool that can help us accomplish our goals and even shapes how we see ourselves. In this chapter, we will explore what money is, where it comes from, and why it's essential to be financially savvy early on in life.

What is money?

Most people think of money as paper bills or coins. And it's true—those are physical representations of money we use to exchange goods and services. But money is more than just pieces of paper or metal.

Money is a tool. It's what we use to buy the things we need (like food, clothing, and shelter) **and pay for services** (like getting a haircut). It's a way to exchange something of value between two people.

> *Think about it like this: When you give someone money for something they are selling, they aren't giving you that item because they care about you—they're exchanging it for something of equal value (money).*

Money comes in different forms, like coins, bills, credit cards, and digital payments. All of these types of money have different values. But no matter the form, money represents a promise of value.

Most countries have their own form of money. In the United States, it's dollars and cents. Other countries, like Canada, Mexico, and Japan, have different types of money with their own names and symbols.

But this wasn't always the case. Let's briefly explore life before money.

. . . .

LIFE BEFORE MONEY

Before money, people used bartering or trading to get what they needed.

Bartering is the act of exchanging a physical good or service for another.

Instead of paying for something with coins or bills, someone would offer goods and services in exchange for other goods or services.

> *For example, if someone had extra apples they wanted to get rid of, they could trade them for something else, like a chicken or a pair of shoes.*

Bartering worked well for small items that had equal value, but it had some significant flaws.

For one, it was hard to compare the value of different items. If a person had a lot of apples but little else, they wouldn't be able to barter for more valuable items like clothing or tools.

Also, trading goods and services could only happen when two people were willing to make the same exchange. What if someone wanted to buy something but didn't have anything the seller wanted in return? That was an issue that bartering couldn't solve.

Money exists because barter is complicated & inefficient

Cutting a cow in half for a box of apples	Accepting two boxes of apples	Selling one cow to two people
= WASTE	**= WASTE**	**= TROUBLE**
= Half a rotting cow	= One box of rotten apples	= Two people arguing

That's why money was created. It allowed people to easily trade for items of different value, no matter what they had to offer in return. It was also a way to store value, making saving up for bigger purchases easier.

A BRIEF HISTORY OF MONEY

Now that you understand bartering, why we use money makes more sense. People invented it so they could get what they needed without needing to barter. But it still took a while before people started using coins and notes.

The History of Money

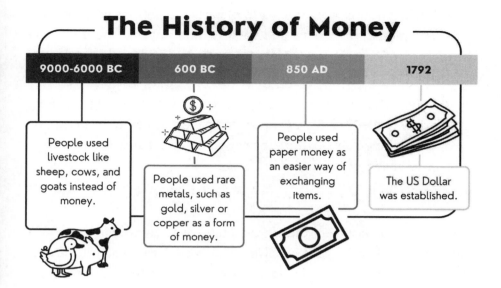

9000-6000 BC	600 BC	850 AD	1792

People used livestock like sheep, cows, and goats instead of money.

People used rare metals, such as gold, silver or copper as a form of money.

People used paper money as an easier way of exchanging items.

The US Dollar was established.

- 9000 BC–6,000 BC. Believe it or not, long ago, people used live-stock like sheep, cows, and goats instead of money. This may not seem like a great solution today (imagine carrying a cow down to the shops to exchange for your groceries!). Still, it was pretty logical in ancient times. These animals were portable and had a value that everyone agreed on.

> **DID YOU KNOW?** In ancient Rome, salt was used as a form of money. The word 'salary" comes from the Latin sal, meaning salt. The term "soldier" means "to be paid in salt," which was how soldiers were paid.

- 600 BC. Another common form of early money was gold or silver. These metals were rare and hard to find, making them valuable currency. Soon, these metals (and others, such as copper) were made into coins of various shapes and sizes.

- 850 AD. Paper money first appeared in China during the Song Dynasty (960–1279 AD). People used paper money as an easier way of exchanging items without having to carry around heavy coins or objects made of metal.

- 1792. The US government officially established the US dollar.

The first paper money in the United States was created in the 1800s, and it was backed by gold or silver. This meant that each dollar was worth a certain amount of gold or silver stored in the US Treasury.

Most countries no longer use gold or silver to back their money. Instead, money is supported by the laws and regulations of the government that created it.

DID YOU KNOW? *Most money isn't physical at all. In the United States, only a tiny portion of the money comprises physical cash. The majority of money today exists only as digital information (numbers on a computer screen). It's a reminder that money isn't just about coins and bills but numbers and transactions.*

10 Key Money Terms

Savings This is the money that you set aside for future use. Savings are a great way to secure your future and build financial security.

Budgeting This is the plan you create to make sure that you spend your money in the most effective way possible. It helps you keep track of your income and expenses so that you can see where your money is going.

Taxes Tax is money you pay to the government. It helps to pay for public services, such as roads and hospitals. Every person is taxed according to the amount of money they earn.

Investing This is when you use your money to purchase something that may increase in value over time. Investing can be a great way to build wealth, but it's essential to understand the risks before you start investing.

Loans Loans are money you borrow from a bank or other lender and have to repay with interest.

Interest **Interest on money you save:** When you save money in a bank account, the bank pays you interest as a reward for keeping your money with them.
Interest on money you borrow: If you borrow money from a bank, you have to pay interest on the amount you borrowed.

Debt This is money you owe someone else, usually a bank or financial institution. This might be in the form of a loan, like a mortgage or a car loan, or something like credit card debt.

Stock Stocks (or shares) are a type of investment where you buy shares in a company. When the company does well, the value usually increases, but when it does poorly, the value might decrease.

Credit Credit is the ability to borrow money from a lender with the promise to pay it back in the future, usually with interest.

Risk This is the possibility of losing money on something. High-risk investments have the potential for high returns but a greater chance of losing money, while low-risk investments typically offer lower returns but may be safer.

CHAPTER 2. BANKING 101

"In banking or finance, trust is the only thing you have to sell."—
Patrick Dixon.

If money makes the world go round, financial institutions like banks
allow this. They make it possible for people to safely store and manage
their money.

Without banks, saving money, investing in the stock market, or borrowing money would be tough.

But as the quote above suggests, when it comes to banking and finance,
the only thing lenders or institutions can offer is trust that they will
handle you and your finances with respect, reliability, and honesty.

DID YOU KNOW? *Banks used to have a policy of complete secrecy.*

*Until the 20th century, banks did not disclose information about
their customers or their accounts, even to law enforcement. This
policy of secrecy was known as "banker's discretion" and was considered essential for maintaining the trust of their customers. Today,
banks must follow strict regulations and reporting requirements.
However, the tradition of discretion and confidentiality is still essential to the banking industry.*

BANK ACCOUNTS - WHAT ARE THEY?
WHY DO YOU NEED ONE?

Imagine if you had to keep all of your money at home. Sure, you could keep it in a safe, under your mattress, or in suitcases. But that would be a lot of work, and it's unsafe. What if there was a flood, fire, or someone broke into your home? Then you'd be out of all of your money!

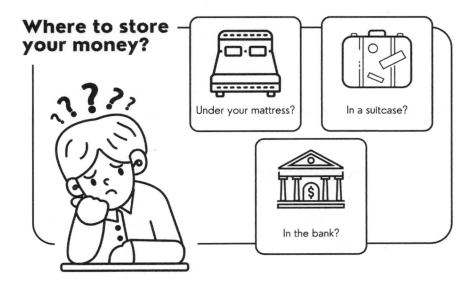

Where to store your money?

Under your mattress?

In a suitcase?

In the bank?

That's why a bank account can be a great option. A bank account is like an online safe to store your money. It's much safer than keeping it at home!

There are other reasons to have a bank account:

- **Convenience:** A bank account makes it easier and more convenient to manage your finances, pay bills, save for the future, and access cash when needed.

- **Accessibility**: Bank accounts are available 24/7, meaning you can access your money whenever needed.

- **Interest income:** You can earn interest on your money if you save it in a savings account. This means that, over time, your money grows.

- **Added security**: Banks help to keep your money safe and secure, protected against theft, loss, or damage.

- **Credit building**: A bank account is one of the first steps to establishing and building a good credit history.

Having a bank account is integral to taking charge of your finances. Now that you know the basics, let's look at how to use one!

. . . .

DIFFERENT TYPES OF ACCOUNTS

When selecting a bank account, different types of accounts are available, depending on your needs. Here are a few of the most common types:

- **Checking account**: A checking account is an excellent option if you need to access your money quickly and frequently. This type of account is mainly used for everyday transactions, like paying bills or buying things with a debit card.

- **Savings account**: A savings account is where you can put your money and earn interest. The interest is a small amount of money that the bank pays you for keeping your money with them. Savings accounts are great for saving up for short-term goals, like a new bike or a trip to the amusement park.

- **Investment account**: An investment account (also known as a brokerage account) is an ideal choice to invest your money and grow your wealth over the long term. This type of account usually offers a variety of investments, such as stocks, bonds, and mutual funds. However, you should know that investments involve risk, so always research before investing.

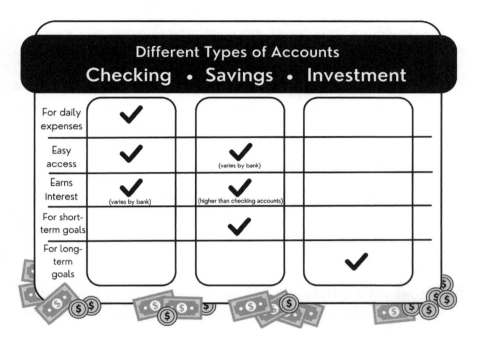

| Different Types of Accounts | | |
Checking	Savings	Investment
For daily expenses	✔		
Easy access	✔	✔ (varies by bank)	
Earns interest	✔ (varies by bank)	✔ (higher than checking accounts)	
For short-term goals		✔	
For long-term goals			✔

OPENING A BANK ACCOUNT IN SIX EASY STEPS

Opening a bank account can be a great way to save money and access various financial services. To open a bank account, follow these six easy steps:

1 **Compare accounts**: Before choosing an account, find one that meets your needs. Consider factors like minimum deposits, account fees, possible interest rates, and features like online banking, debit cards, and mobile applications. Some banks might even offer special promotions or discounts for students.

2 **Gather required documents**: To open a bank account, you must provide a valid form of identification, such as a driver's license, passport, or birth certificate. If you're under 18, you might need an adult to help verify your identity and provide proof of your address. You should check with the bank to see what documents they require.

3 **Choose a bank**: Once you've compared accounts and gathered the necessary documents, it's time to choose one. You can look for banks with branches or ATMs near your home or school. You might also consider banks with mobile applications, good customer reviews, or rewards programs.

4 **Open the account**: You'll need to fill out an application to open the account. This can typically be done online or in person. Make sure you double-check your information before submitting the application.

5 **Fund the account**: Once your account is open, you will need to fund it. You can do this by transferring money from another account or depositing cash.

6 **Activate the account**: If you open the account online, the bank will usually send you an email or text message with a link to activate your account. Once you have activated your account, you can access it online or through the bank's mobile app.

Following these steps should make it easy to open a bank account. Once you're all set up, you can safely store your money and take advantage of the other services the bank offers. But before you do, there are a few other things you'll need to know to manage your money effectively. One important thing to keep track of is your bank statement.

BANK STATEMENTS

Your bank statement lists all transactions made on your account, including deposits, withdrawals, payments, etc.

Bank statements used to be mailed out to customers monthly or quarterly, but now most banks offer digital statements that can be viewed online. Reviewing your bank statement regularly is a good habit to ensure the transactions are accurate and to keep track of your spending.

STATEMENT FROM JANUARY 1-15, 2023			ACCOUNT 123456789
DATE	DEPOSITS	WITHDRAWALS	BALANCE
JAN02	1000.00		
JAN05		100.00	900.00
JAN10		215.00	685.00
JAN12	157.50		842.50
JAN14	500.50		1343.00
TOTAL	1658.00	315.00	1343.00

Here's a quick guide to reviewing your statement:

1 **Check the balance:** The first thing to check is your account balance. This is the amount of money you have in your account. Ensure it matches what you expect and that you have enough money to cover upcoming payments.

2 **Review transactions:** Go through each transaction in your statement to ensure accuracy. If you see a transaction you don't recognize, it could be a mistake or an instance of fraud. Contact your bank as soon as possible if you suspect any errors.

3 **Check for fees:** Make sure you understand the costs associated with your account. Some standard fees include overdraft fees, monthly maintenance fees, and fees for using ATMs outside your bank's network. Contact your bank for more information if you need clarification on a fee.

4 **Monitor account activity:** Regularly reviewing your bank statement is an excellent way to monitor your spending. Seeing your transactions in one place can help you stick to a budget and identify areas where you can reduce spending.

By following these steps, you can ensure your bank account is in good standing, and your finances are on track.

UNDERSTANDING TRANSACTIONS

When reviewing the activity on your account, it's helpful to understand the different types of payments on your account.

- **Direct Debits:** A direct debit is an agreement between you and a company to automatically deduct a certain amount from your bank account each month. This type of payment is commonly used for bills such as utility bills, phone bills, and insurance premiums. With direct debits, you won't have to worry about missing a payment or incurring late fees because the payments are automatically made for you.

- **Standing Orders:** A standing order is similar to a direct debit, but it is usually used to transfer a fixed amount each month rather than a variable amount. *For example, you might set up a standing order to pay your rent or monthly gym membership each month.*

- **Recurring Payments:** Recurring payments are similar to direct debits and standing orders, but they're made through cards like credit and debit cards, and the transactions will appear in your statement as "recurring" or "subscription." *For example, let's say you subscribe to a video streaming service like Netflix. Netflix will automatically charge your debit or credit card for the subscription fee every month. You don't have to do anything; it happens automatically.*

- **Bank Transfers:** A bank transfer is a payment you make from one bank account to another. Bank transfers can be made online, over the phone, or at a bank branch. You will need the recipient's bank account information, including their account number and sort code, to make a bank transfer. Bank transfers are typically processed within a few working days.

- **Card Payments:** A card payment is a payment made using a debit or credit card. Card payments can be made in person, online, or over the phone. Card payments are processed almost instantly and are a convenient way to pay for goods and services. When you make a card payment, the money is deducted from your bank account (if you use a debit card) or from your credit card limit (if you use a credit card).

It's also important to look out for any charges or fees that you don't recognize. This could be an indication of fraudulent activity on your account. If you see any suspicious transactions, contact your bank immediately.

Accessing your Money

ATM

Most banks have ATMs you can use to withdraw cash from your account. Some ATMs are only for customers of the bank, while others are part of a network that customers of different banks can use.

Debit Card

Most bank accounts come with a debit card that can be used to withdraw cash from ATMs or make purchases at merchants that accept debit cards.

Online Banking

Most banks offer online banking services that allow you to view your account information and make transactions online. You can also use online banking to transfer money between your bank accounts or to pay bills.

Mobile Banking

Many banks offer mobile banking apps you can download to your smartphone. These apps allow you to access your account information and make transactions on the go.

In-Person Banking

Some banks have branches where you can go to speak with a customer representative in person. You can also deposit cash or checks at these branches.

ACCESSING YOUR MONEY

Once you've set up your bank account and are equipped with the skills and knowledge to manage it effectively, you'll need to know how to access your money. There are several ways to access your money, depending on your needs and the services offered by your bank. Here are a few common options:

- **ATM:** Most banks have ATMs that you can use to withdraw cash from your account. Some ATMs are only for bank customers, while others are part of a network that can be used by customers of different banks.

- **Debit card:** Most bank accounts come with a debit card that can be used to withdraw cash from ATMs or make purchases at merchants that accept debit cards.

- **Online banking:** Most banks offer online banking services allowing you to view your account information and transact online. You can also use online banking to transfer money between your bank accounts or to pay bills.

- **Mobile banking:** Many banks offer mobile banking apps you can download. These apps allow you to access your account information and make transactions on the go.

- **In-person banking:** Some banks have branches where you can speak with a customer service representative. You can also deposit cash or checks at these branches.

By understanding the different ways to access your money, you can choose the best methods for you and your lifestyle.

> **DID YOU KNOW?** The first ATM (automated teller machine) was installed in London in 1967!

CHAPTER 3. CREDIT REPORTS—
WHY YOUR CREDIT SCORE MATTERS!

In this chapter, we'll be talking about credit reports.

Credit reports may not be the most exciting thing in the world—in fact, they can seem pretty dull and unimportant at first glance. But they're actually super important and will play a big role in your financial life as you get older.

. . . .

BUT FIRST UP, WHAT IS CREDIT?

Credit refers to the ability to borrow money or receive goods or services now and pay for them later. Individuals, businesses, or financial institutions, such as banks and credit card companies, can extend credit.

When you use credit, you are borrowing money that you will have to pay back later, usually with interest.

> *For example, when you use a credit card to make a purchase, you are borrowing money from the credit card company, and you will have to pay back the borrowed amount plus any interest charges.*

Credit can also be used to purchase big-ticket items such as cars, home appliances, or even a home. This is called installment credit and is a loan that's paid back over a period of time, usually with interest.

Credit can be helpful in many ways. It allows people to buy things they need or want without paying for them all at once. But it's essential to use credit responsibly and make payments on time; otherwise, it can lead to debt and negatively impact your credit score.

WHAT IS A CREDIT REPORT?

A credit report is a document prepared by a credit reporting agency that shows your credit history. It's like a report card for your finances, showing how well you've handled credit in the past. This information is used by lenders, landlords, and other people or organizations to decide whether or not to give you credit or to approve you for a loan or rental property.

Every time you apply for a credit card, loan, or any other type of credit, the lender will check your credit report to see how responsible you've been with credit in the past. Your credit report will show information such as:

- Your credit accounts, including credit cards, loans, and mortgages
- How much credit you have been given
- How much credit you are currently using
- How promptly you have paid your bills
- Any late payments or defaults on your credit accounts
- Any bankruptcies or legal judgments against you

CREDIT REPORTS VS. CREDIT SCORES – WHAT'S THE DIFFERENCE?

Your credit report and credit score are related but not the same thing.

Your credit report is a detailed document that shows your credit history.

Your credit score, on the other hand, is a numerical value that is calculated based on the information in your credit report. It's a snapshot of your creditworthiness, and it's used by lenders to decide whether or not to approve you for credit. Credit scores are generally between 300 and 850. The higher your score, the better your creditworthiness.

WHY A GOOD CREDIT SCORE MATTERS & WHY YOU SHOULD CARE!

Even though you may not have the need for credit in the near future, it's important to start thinking about your credit score now because the choices you make with your money today will impact your credit score.

Here are a few reasons why having a good credit score matters:

- **Access to credit:** A good credit score will make it easier to get approved for credit in the future. This includes credit cards, car loans, student loans, and mortgages. When you have a good credit score, lenders see you as a lower risk, and they are more likely to approve you for credit.

- **Lower interest rates:** When you have a good credit score, you'll be offered lower interest rates on loans and credit cards. This means you'll save money on interest charges over time.

- **Better rental options:** Landlords often check credit reports when you apply to rent a property. A good credit score can make you more likely to be approved for a rental.

- **Job opportunities:** Some employers check credit reports as part of the hiring process. A good credit score can help you get the job you want.

- **Insurance:** A good credit score can also help you get lower rates on insurance, such as car insurance.

- **Building good habits:** Building good credit takes time; the earlier you start, the better. Learning how to manage your credit responsibly now is essential so you'll be prepared when you need it in the future.

Think of it like planting a seed in a garden. It takes time and effort to grow, but the end result is a beautiful and healthy plant. Building a good credit score is similar. It takes time and effort, but the result is a solid financial foundation that will benefit you in the long run.

BUT WHAT DOES IT MEAN IN REALITY?

Let's say you want to buy a car. You've saved up enough money for a down payment and are ready to start looking for car loans.

If you have a good credit score — say around 700 or above — lenders will likely see you as a low-risk borrower. They'll be more willing to lend you money, and you'll probably qualify for a lower interest rate on your loan. This means you'll pay less in interest over the life of the loan, and you'll be able to afford a more expensive car.

On the other hand, if your credit score is low — let's say around 600 or below — lenders will see you as a high-risk borrower. They'll be less likely to lend you money, and you'll likely be offered a higher interest rate on your loan. This means you'll pay more in interest over the life of the loan, and you may not be able to afford the car you want.

Credit Risk

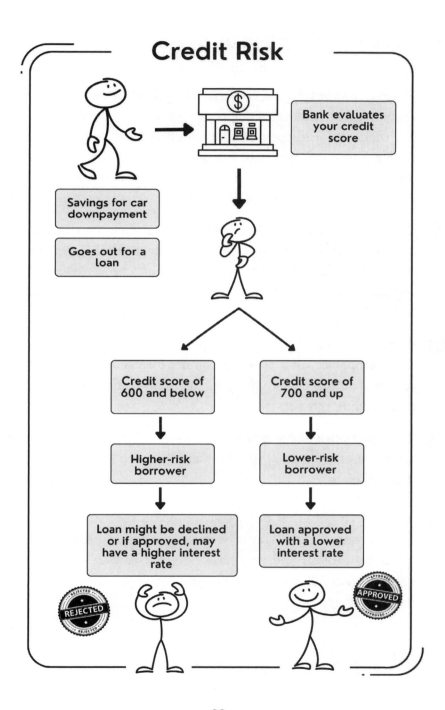

HOW YOU CAN CHECK YOUR CREDIT SCORE

There are a few ways you can check your credit score:

1 **Credit reporting agencies:** The US's three major credit reporting agencies are Equifax, Experian, and TransUnion. You can request a free copy of your credit report from each agency once a year by visiting their websites or calling them. Your credit report will show you the agency's information on file for you, but it will not include your credit score.

2 **Online credit score providers**: Several online providers offer free credit score checking. These providers will give you a credit score based on the information in your credit report. Some popular online providers include Credit Karma, Credit Sesame, and Quizzle.

3 **Banks and credit card companies**: Some banks and credit card companies offer their customers free access to their credit scores. You can check with your bank or credit card company if they provide this service.

4 **Credit counseling services**: Some credit counseling services will provide you with your credit score for free as part of their services.

It's important to note that the credit score you receive from different sources may vary slightly. This is because it is determined by different credit scoring models and may have different ranges. However, the score should generally be close enough to give you an idea of where you stand.

FACTORS THAT AFFECT YOUR SCORE

Your credit score is based on the information in your credit report. The five most significant factors that affect your credit are:

① **Payment history:** This is the most crucial factor, making up about 35% of your credit score. It reflects how good you are at paying your bills on time. Late payments, collections, and bankruptcy will hurt your score, while on-time payments will improve it.

② **Credit utilization:** This factor makes up about 30% of your credit score and refers to how much credit you're using compared to how much you have available. The more you use (*for example, using a lot of your credit card limit*) the lower your score. In comparison, using less of your available credit will help improve it.

③ **Length of credit history:** This makes up about 15% of your credit score and reflects the age of your credit accounts and how long you've been using credit. The longer your credit history, the better—as long as you have a good track record of paying on time.

④ **Credit mix:** This factor makes up about 10% of your credit score and refers to the different types of credit you have, such as credit cards, loans, and mortgages. A mix of credit types can be helpful for your score—as long as you're making payments on time.

⑤ **New credit:** This factor makes up about 10% of your credit score and refers to how many new credit applications you've made recently. Every time you apply for new credit, it can affect your credit score, so it's best to limit the number of new applications you make.

By understanding these factors, you can work to improve your credit score.

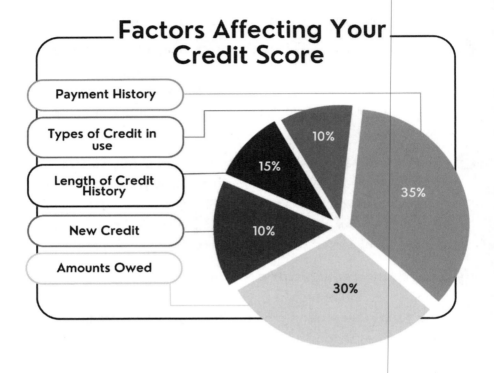

Factors Affecting Your Credit Score

- Payment History
- Types of Credit in use
- Length of Credit History
- New Credit
- Amounts Owed

10%
15%
35%
10%
30%

- -

HOW YOU CAN MAINTAIN A GOOD CREDIT SCORE OR IMPROVE YOUR CREDIT SCORE

Knowing the basics of how credit works can help you manage it properly. There are no shortcuts to improving your credit score, just good financial behavior.

Here are some general tips for maintaining a good score or improving your score:

1. **Pay your bills on time:** This is the most important thing you can do to keep your credit score healthy. Make sure you pay all

of your bills by their due date so that you don't fall behind and get hit with late fees.

2 **Keep your credit card balances low:** If you have a credit card, try not to use up too much of your available credit. Keeping your balances low shows lenders that you're responsible with your money.

3 **Don't apply for too much credit at once:** Every time you apply for a new credit card or loan, it can temporarily lower your credit score. Try not to apply for too many things at once, or it could hurt your score.

4 **Check your credit report regularly:** Your credit report shows all of the accounts that are open in your name and any missed payments or other negative marks. Make sure to check it every year to make sure everything looks right.

5 **Ask for help if you need it:** If you're having trouble paying off debts or keeping up with bills, don't be afraid to ask for help from a parent or trusted adult. They might be able to advise you on managing your money better.

6 **Don't close old accounts:** If you have an old account you no longer use, don't rush to close it! Closing an account can hurt your score because it shortens the length of time that you've had credit.

7 **Be patient:** Building good credit takes time! Don't worry if things aren't perfect immediately—just keep making good choices, and your score will improve over time.

It's important to note that there's no instant way to improve your credit profile. It takes time and effort to do so. However, by following these tips and being responsible with credit, you can improve your credit profile over time.

DID YOU KNOW? *Individuals and businesses aren't the only ones to borrow money. Governments also borrow money to fund essential projects or infrastructure improvements. In fact, as of February 2023, the U.S. national debt was over 31 trillion dollars!*

CHAPTER 4. JOBS & MONEY

> **DID YOU KNOW?** *The average person spends 90,000 hours working in their lifetime!*

Work is changing fast, and it's becoming more common for people to change jobs multiple times throughout their careers. The rise of the gig economy, remote work, and the increasing demand for specialized skills are some of the factors that are contributing to this trend.

The average person today will have 11-15 jobs during their lifetime. This means they must adapt to new roles and responsibilities, learn new skills, and build new professional networks.

That's why it's essential to be adaptable, open to new opportunities, and always willing to learn.

This chapter is designed to give you a solid foundation for understanding the world of jobs and money to prepare you for the ever-changing job market. It will help you be more informed and confident about your finances and better prepared for the world of work when you are ready to join the workforce. Whether you're thinking about your first job or already working and looking to improve your finances, this chapter will provide you with the information you need to make smart decisions about your money and be ready for the opportunities that come your way.

Before we delve into the world of work, let's quickly look through some key terms you'll be hearing:

Different Types of Employment Status

Employed	A person who works for a company or organization and receives a salary or wage in exchange for their services. E.g. a waiter at a restaurant or an attorney at a law firm.
Self-employed	A person who runs their own business and is responsible for managing all aspects of it, including finances, marketing, and operations.
Full-time	An employee who works a set number of hours per week, typically 35-40 hours, and is eligible for benefits such as health insurance and paid time off.
Part-time	A job that typically requires an employee to work fewer hours per week, usually less than 35 hours.
Temporary	A job that is offered for a specific period of time, usually to cover for a leave of absence, seasonal work or special projects.
Freelance	A type of self-employment that allows a person to work independently and choose their own clients and projects.

- **Employed:** When a person is working for an employer, typically on a regular schedule and receiving a salary or wages. This could be anything from being a waiter at a restaurant to an attorney at a law firm.

- **Self-employed:** When people work for themselves, typically as independent contractors or freelancers. They are responsible for their own taxes and benefits.

- **Full-time:** A job that typically requires an employee to work at least 35–40 hours per week.

- **Part-time:** A job that typically requires an employee to work fewer hours per week, usually less than 35 hours.

- **Temporary:** A job offered for a specific period, usually to cover a leave of absence, seasonal work, or special projects.

- **Freelance:** A type of self-employment that allows people to work independently and choose their clients and projects.

Each type of employment has pros and cons, and understanding them is helpful before deciding what type of work is best for you.

. . . .

EMPLOYED VS. SELF-EMPLOYED

Whether you work for yourself or someone else is a personal decision that depends on your needs, preferences, and circumstances. Some people prefer the stability and benefits of being an employee. Whilst others enjoy the freedom and earning potential of being self-employed. Both types of employment have unique challenges and rewards, and it's wise to consider your values, skills, and goals when deciding.

Here are some pros and cons to consider:

Employed

Pros:

- Consistent income: As an employee, you will typically receive a regular salary or hourly wage.

- Benefits: Many employers offer health insurance, retirement plans, paid time off, and more.

- Job security: Being an employee means you have a contract with your employer, which provides some level of job security.

What's Right For You?

	Employed	Self-Employed
PROS 	• Regular salary and benefits, such as health insurance and retirement plans • Opportunities for advancement and career growth • Structured work environment and support from colleagues • Job security and stability • Less responsibility for business operations and taxes	• Greater control over work schedule and projects • Ability to pursue passions and interests • Potential for higher income and tax deductions • Greater flexibility in work location and environment • Opportunity to build a business and work with a variety of clients
CONS 	• Less control over work schedule and projects • Limited opportunity to pursue passions and interests • Potential for limited income growth • Limited flexibility in work location and environment • Potential for office politics and conflict with colleagues.	• Uncertain income and potential for financial stress • Responsibility for all aspects of business operations • Lack of benefits, such as health insurance and retirement plans • Limited opportunities for advancement or career growth

- Professional development: Employers often provide training and development opportunities for their employees to improve their skills and advance in their careers.

- Structure: Employers usually have established systems and processes that employees can rely on.

Cons:

- Limited autonomy: As an employee, you will likely have to follow a set of guidelines and procedures set by your employer.

- Limited earning potential: Your earning potential may be capped by your employer's salary structure or budget.

- Lack of flexibility: Employers usually expect employees to be available during set working hours.

Self-employed

Pros:

- Autonomy: As a self-employed person, you have more control over your work schedule, clients, and projects.

- Unlimited earning potential: Your earning potential is not limited by an employer's salary structure or budget.

- Flexibility: You can work the hours that suit you.

- Variety: You can take on various clients and projects, making your work more diverse and exciting.

Cons:

- Uncertain income: As a self-employed person, your income may be inconsistent and depend on the availability of clients and projects.

- No benefits: As a self-employed person, you are responsible for your own benefits, such as health insurance and retirement savings.

- Job insecurity: You have to constantly look for new clients and projects to maintain a steady income.

- No structure: Self-employed people have to create their own systems and processes, which can be time-consuming and overwhelming.

It's important to weigh the pros and cons of each type of employment before making a decision.

EMPLOYABILITY AND EARNING POTENTIAL

You might have heard people talk about your earning potential. Earning potential refers to the amount of money you can make in your career based on your education, skills, experience, and other factors. It is an estimate of what you might earn in the future and is influenced by several variables. Some of the critical factors that can impact your earning potential include:

1. **Education:** A higher level of education can often lead to higher-paying jobs, as many employers are looking for workers with specialized skills and knowledge.

2. **Work experience:** Having work experience in your field or related fields can help increase your earning potential. This is because you have demonstrated your ability to perform well on the job and have developed skills and expertise that are valuable to employers.

3 **Industry:** The industry you work in can also impact your earning potential. Some industries, such as technology, finance, and medicine, tend to offer higher salaries than others.

4 **Location:** The cost of living and the average salaries in a particular area can also impact your earning potential. For example, workers in cities with a high cost of living may need to earn more to cover their expenses.

5 **Skills and talents:** Having unique skills or talents can also increase your earning potential. They can help you stand out from other job applicants and command a higher salary.

It's important to note that these are just a few factors that can impact earning potential.

It's also important to recognize that earning potential is not the only measure of success or happiness. In fact, money is just one of many vital aspects of a happy and fulfilling life. Many other factors contribute to a person's overall well-being and a sense of purpose, including relationships, health, hobbies and interests, community involvement, and personal growth and development.

While a high-earning job can help you achieve your financial goals, it doesn't guarantee happiness or financial stability. Having a good work-life balance, living in a low-cost area, and having a solid support network can all play a role in helping you achieve financial stability and security.

Ultimately, it's important to find a balance that works for you, considering your values, priorities, and financial goals and needs.

EVERYTHING YOU NEED TO KNOW ABOUT PAYCHECKS

Congratulations, you've gotten your first paycheck! This is an exciting milestone in your journey toward financial independence. But before you go out and spend all your hard-earned money, it's important to understand what's included in your paycheck.

Paycheck

Jane's Business
123 Main Street
Nowhere, USA 00000

Week of April 2-6, 2022
Joe Employee
123-45-6789

Gross Pay **$500**
Deductions

1. Federal Tax . . . . -68.00
2. State Tax . . . . -64.00
3. Social Security . . . . -31.00
4. Medicare . . . . -7.25

Net ————————————————————————————— **$329.75**

WHAT IS A PAYCHECK AND WHY IS IT IMPORTANT?

A paycheck is a document showing the amount of money you've earned for your work. Your paycheck shows how much money you earned from your job and how much was taken out for taxes, health insurance, retirement plans, and other deductions.

It is also called a salary slip, pay stub or payslip.

As an employee, it's essential to understand and review your paycheck and ensure the information is correct, including your gross pay, deductions, and net pay. If you notice any errors, contact your employer and have them corrected.

· ·

CALCULATING YOUR PAY – GROSS VS. NET

Your paycheck will typically include your gross and net pay.

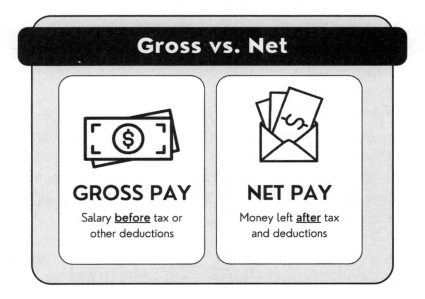

Gross vs. Net

GROSS PAY
Salary **before** tax or other deductions

NET PAY
Money left **after** tax and deductions

Gross pay is the total money you've earned before taxes and deductions.

Net pay is how much money you take home. This is the amount of money you have left after all deductions and taxes have been removed. This is the money you will have available to use for expenses, savings, and investments.

TAX - WHERE DID ALL THE MONEY GO?

Taxes can be a confusing and sometimes frustrating part of earning money. Seeing a large portion of your paycheck go towards taxes can be disheartening. Still, it's important to remember that taxes are a necessary part of our society. They help fund essential services such as schools, roads, and health care.

When you earn money, a percentage is withheld from your paycheck to go towards federal and state income taxes and other taxes such as Social Security and Medicare. The amount withheld depends on your income level, filing status, and any deductions or credits you may qualify for.

WHO PAYS TAXES?

Not everyone pays taxes. Tax laws vary from country to country, but taxes are usually based on a person's income and assets. Some people may not have to pay taxes because they do not earn enough money to reach the minimum income threshold, while others may be eligible for tax exemptions or credits that reduce their tax liability.

In some countries, certain groups of people don't have to pay taxes, such as students, disabled individuals, and veterans. Additionally, certain types of income, such as gifts and inheritance, may not be subject to taxes.

However, most people who earn an income and meet specific criteria must pay taxes. This includes employed and self-employed people and those who receive money from investments and rental properties.

It's also worth noting that taxes aren't just on income. Different types of taxes, such as sales tax, property tax, and others, may apply to an individual or a business.

CHAPTER 5. KEEPING IT PRIVATE—

FRAUDS AND SCAMS

Fraud and scams are unfortunately common in today's world. These crimes occur when someone uses deceit or trickery to take money or personal information from unsuspecting individuals.

Fraud can come in many forms, from online scams to phone scams. It can target anyone, regardless of age, income, or education level. It's important to be aware of the different types of fraud and scams and to take steps to protect yourself and your personal information from fraud.

In this chapter, we'll cover fraud and scams, how they work, and what you should look out for. We'll also discuss how to protect yourself and your personal information from fraud and scams and what to do if you suspect you've been a victim.

· ·

WHAT ARE FRAUD AND SCAMS, AND WHY DO PEOPLE DO IT?

Fraud and scams are criminal activities that involve deceiving or tricking people into taking their money or personal information. Fraudsters and scammers use a variety of tactics to trick people, such as using fake websites, emails, phone calls, or social media messages to steal personal information or money.

People do it because they think they can get away with it and make money without doing any real work. Unfortunately, fraudsters often target vulnerable people who are desperate for cash or looking for an easy way out of their problems.

There are many different types of fraud and scams. It's essential to be aware of these scams and take steps to protect yourself from them.

> **DID YOU KNOW?** *According to the Federal Trade Commission (FTC), individuals in the US lost $5.8 billion to fraud in 2021.*

Examples of online scams include:

- **The Nigerian Prince Scam**

    The Nigerian Prince scam is a type of fraud where someone sends you an email claiming to be a wealthy prince from Nigeria. The email says that the prince needs your help to transfer his money out of the country and promises to give you a large portion of the money if you help him. However, once you agree to help, the scammers will ask for personal information or money to cover "fees" or "taxes" related to the transfer. In reality, there is no prince and no money—it's all just a scam to trick people into giving away their hard-earned money.

    This scam is also called an "advance-fee scam" because the scammers ask for money upfront.

- **The Imposter Scam**

    The Imposter scam is similar to the Nigerian Prince scam, but instead of someone claiming to be an actual prince, they pretend to be someone you know and trust, like a friend or family member. They might create a fake social media account or email address and contact you, saying they're in trouble and need money urgently. They'll ask you to wire money or give them your credit card information, but it's all a lie—the person pretending to be your friend or family member is a scammer trying to steal your money.

You might think you'll never fall for a scam, but it's important to remember that scammers are super smart. They are becoming more sophisticated in their tactics and are constantly coming up with new ways to trick people. They may use convincing language, official-looking documents, and even fake websites and social media accounts to make their scams seem real.

· ·
WHAT STEPS CAN YOU TAKE TO AVOID BECOMING A VICTIM OF FRAUD?

Now that you have a better understanding of the tactics scammers use to trick people into giving them money or sensitive information, let's look at some of the steps you can take to avoid becoming a victim of fraud:

1. **Keep your personal information private:** Don't share your personal information, such as full name, address, phone number, email, or social security number, with anyone you don't know or trust.

2. **Be cautious when using public Wi-Fi:** Public Wi-Fi is often unsecured and easily hacked. Avoid making financial transactions or entering sensitive information while using public Wi-Fi.

3. **Use strong passwords:** Create strong passwords that include letters, numbers, and special characters for your online accounts. Avoid reusing passwords across multiple accounts.

Frauds & Scams

There are many different types of fraud and scams, some examples include:

Phishing Scams
These are a type of cyber attack where scammers attempt to get hold of sensitive information such as usernames, passwords, and credit card details. This is often done through fraudulent emails or websites that appear to be legitimate.

Investment Scams
These scams involve fraudsters who create fake businesses that trick people into giving them money by promising big returns. But in reality, these people just take the money and run.

Lottery Scams
These scams involve fraudsters who tell people they've won a large sum of money, but in order to claim the prize, they need personal information or bank account details to process the payment.

Work-from-home Scams
These scams involve fraudsters who promise people the opportunity to make money from home, but in reality, the job is non-existent, or the employer is not real. They may ask for personal information or money as part of the application.

Romance Scams
These scams involve fraudsters who create fake online profiles and pretend to be interested in a romantic relationship, in order to gain trust and steal money or personal information from the victim.

Charity Scams
These scams involve fraudsters who pretend to be a charity and ask for donations to help a cause, but in reality, they keep the money for themselves.

Online Shopping Scams
Scammers create fake websites that look like real online stores, but when people make a purchase, they don't receive the item and lose their money.

Identity Theft Scams
Scammers steal personal information, such as a person's name, address, or social security number, and uses it to open credit cards or take out loans in that name.

4. **Don't click on suspicious links:** If you receive an email or message with a suspicious link, do not click on it. It could be a phishing scam designed to steal your personal information.

5. **Double-check before giving out personal information:** Always double-check the identity of the person asking for your personal data through another means of communication before giving it out.

6. **Monitor your bank accounts:** Regularly check your bank accounts for any unusual activity.

7. **Don't send money to strangers:** Never wire money to someone you don't know or trust, especially if they urgently ask for it.

8. **Be wary of offers that seem too good to be true:** Scammers often use offers that seem too good to be true, such as winning the lottery! Unfortunately, if it sounds too good to be true, it probably is.

9. **Report suspicious activity:** If you suspect someone is trying to scam you, report it to the authorities immediately.

10. **Educate yourself about different types of fraud:** Stay informed about different types of fraud so that you can recognize them when they occur and take appropriate action to protect yourself.

Following these suggestions can significantly reduce your risk of falling victim to fraud or scams. Remember to always be cautious, do your research, and trust your instincts. By staying informed and vigilant, you can better protect yourself and your finances from fraud and scams.

WHAT TO DO IF YOU THINK YOU'VE BEEN SCAMMED?

If you've fallen victim to a scam, it's important to remember that it's not your fault. Scammers are experts at finding new ways to trick people, and it's not uncommon to be scammed. Unfortunately, you are not the first person it has happened to, so don't be too hard on yourself. Instead, focus on the steps to report the scam and recover what you can.

If you suspect that you have fallen victim to a scam, there are a few steps you should take immediately:

1. **Don't send any more money to the scammer:** This may sound obvious, but once you realize you have been scammed, stop all financial transactions with the scammer. Scammers can be very persuasive and may try to convince you to make additional payments.

2. **Contact your bank:** Tell them what happened and ask them to freeze your account or cancel any unauthorized transactions.

3. **Report the fraud:** Contact relevant authorities, such as the US Federal Trade Commission (FTC) or Action Fraud in the UK. They will help you report the incident and provide guidance on how to proceed.

4. **Gather evidence:** Collect any documentation, emails, or messages related to the scam. This will be useful when you file a report or make a claim.

5. **Don't pay for recovery:** If a scammer tells you to pay them to recover your money, don't do it. Scammers often ask for payment to trick you into giving them more of your money.

6 **Take care of your emotional well-being:** Scams can be traumatic, and taking the time to process the experience and care for yourself is important.

7 **Learn from it:** As painful and unpleasant being scammed is, try your best to learn from what happened to keep yourself safe in the future.

Unfortunately, not every scam can be stopped or recovered from. But remember that it's not your fault you've been scammed, and try to learn from the experience to avoid future scams.

PART TWO:

BUDGETING AND SAVVY SPENDING

CHAPTER 6. BUDGETING – MAKING A PLAN (AND STICKING TO IT)

In this chapter, we'll dive into the world of spending habits and budgeting. We'll start by looking at different spender personalities, so you can understand your own spending habits and how to make them work for you. We'll also cover the importance of creating a budget and how to make one that works for you. We'll talk about the difference between needs and wants and how to ensure you spend your money on what truly matters. Finally, we'll introduce the 50/30/20 rule, a simple way to ensure you save enough for your future. By the end of this chapter, you'll better understand how to manage your money and make it work for you.

WHAT KIND OF SPENDER ARE YOU?

Everyone has their own unique way of spending and managing their money. Understanding your own spending personality can help you make better financial decisions.

Here are a few examples of spending personalities:

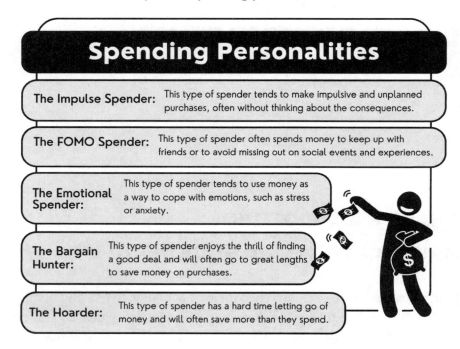

Spending Personalities

The Impulse Spender: This type of spender tends to make impulsive and unplanned purchases, often without thinking about the consequences.

The FOMO Spender: This type of spender often spends money to keep up with friends or to avoid missing out on social events and experiences.

The Emotional Spender: This type of spender tends to use money as a way to cope with emotions, such as stress or anxiety.

The Bargain Hunter: This type of spender enjoys the thrill of finding a good deal and will often go to great lengths to save money on purchases.

The Hoarder: This type of spender has a hard time letting go of money and will often save more than they spend.

- **The impulse spender:** This type of spender tends to make impulsive and unplanned purchases, often without thinking about the consequences.

- **The FOMO spender:** This type of spender often spends money to keep up with friends or to avoid missing out on social events and experiences.

- **The emotional spender:** This type of spender tends to use money as a way to cope with emotions, such as stress or anxiety.

- **The bargain hunter:** This type of spender enjoys finding a good deal and often goes to great lengths to save money on purchases.

- **The hoarder:** This type of spender has difficulty letting go of money and will often save more than they spend.

By understanding your spending personality, you can make more conscious and deliberate spending decisions and ensure that your spending habits align with your financial goals.

THE IMPULSE SPENDER

The impulse spender tends to make impulsive purchases without thinking about the financial consequences. They might see something they like and buy it without considering whether they can afford it or need it. They often have difficulty resisting sales and discounts and may struggle to stick to a budget. However, this spender personality can also be spontaneous and fun-loving and may enjoy the thrill of the purchase.

THE FOMO SPENDER

The FOMO (fear of missing out) spender is someone who spends money because they don't want to miss out on experiences or opportunities. They feel a sense of pressure to keep up with others, whether it's the latest fashion trends, gadgets, or social events. They are always looking for new experiences and tend to be impulsive when spending. They may also have trouble saying no to friends and family regarding social activities involving spending money. This type of spending can lead to financial stress and difficulty sticking to a budget, as they may not be considering the long-term financial consequences of their spending decisions.

• •

THE EMOTIONAL SPENDER

The emotional spender is someone who uses shopping and spending as a way to cope with their emotions. They may turn to shopping as a form of stress relief or use it as a way to celebrate or reward themselves. They may not be aware that their spending is out of control or connected to their emotions. They may also have difficulty saying no to themselves or others or find themselves constantly buying things they don't need. This type of spending can lead to financial problems and debt if not addressed. Emotional spenders need to learn how to manage their emotions and create a budget to help them stay on track.

• •

THE BARGAIN HUNTER

The bargain hunter loves finding a good deal and always looks for discounts and sales. They enjoy the thrill of the hunt and seek ways to stretch their money further. They often have a keen eye for detail and can spot a good deal from a mile away. They are skilled at comparison shopping and can usually find the same item for a much lower price than others might pay. However, they may also have a tendency to overspend on things they don't really need just because they are a good deal. It's crucial for bargain hunters to set a budget, stick to it, and make sure they only spend money on things they truly need and value.

THE HOARDER

The hoarder is a type of spender who has difficulty letting go of their possessions, whether physical items or money. They may have trouble spending money on things they need or want and may hold onto items even if they no longer have any use for them. They often feel secure in having a lot of money or possessions and may struggle to part with them. This type of spending behavior can lead to financial stress and clutter in their home or life. Hoarders need to understand their behavior and work on developing healthier spending habits, such as setting a budget and learning to prioritize their needs and wants.

Of course, there are many other spending personality types, and you may identify with more than one. The important thing is to understand your own spending habits and how they affect your financial goals. Once you know your spending personality, you can work on creating a budget that works for you and your lifestyle.

AN INTRODUCTION TO BUDGETING

Budgeting is the simplest way to take control of your money. A budget is a financial plan that considers all the money you will make over a certain period and how much you're likely to spend. You make the plan, and then you stick to it.

What is the basic aim of budgeting? To try and control your spending. The ultimate goal? To spend less money than you make.

This may sound simple. How do you, after all, spend money you don't have? But many people do this each month, relying on credit cards, loans, or overdrafts to allow them to spend money they haven't yet earned.

Think of budgeting like driving a car—you need to know where you're headed and how much gas you have in the tank to make it to your destination safely and efficiently. Just like you need to plan your route and monitor your fuel levels, you also need to plan your income and expenses to ensure you're on the right track financially.

Remember, budgeting is about controlling your money instead of your money controlling you.

DID YOU KNOW? *Budgeting is good for your health. By taking control of your finances and setting clear goals for your spending, budgeting can reduce stress and increase feelings of security and well-being. In fact, studies have shown that people who regularly practice budgeting are more likely to have higher levels of life satisfaction and a more positive outlook on their financial future.*

NEEDS VS. WANTS...

You might want that new laptop, but do you really need it?

Understanding the difference between needs and wants is an essential part of budgeting.

"Needs" are essential items or services that are required for survival, such as food, shelter, and clothing.

"Wants" are things that are desired or desirable but not essential. They are often luxuries or things that would make life more comfortable or convenient but that are not necessary for survival, such as a new laptop or a vacation.

Being able to distinguish between needs and wants can help you make more informed financial decisions and prioritize where to allocate your money.

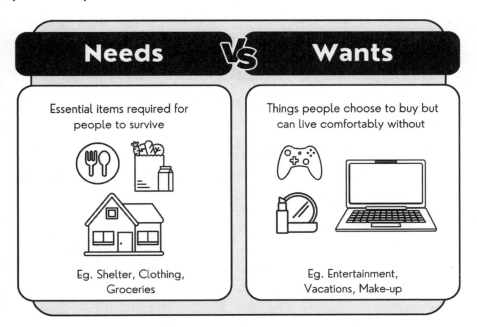

Needs	Wants
Essential items required for people to survive	Things people choose to buy but can live comfortably without
Eg. Shelter, Clothing, Groceries	Eg. Entertainment, Vacations, Make-up

For example, having a fancy car or designer clothes may be a want, but having a reliable means of transportation to get to work or school is a need.

HOW TO BUDGET IN 5 SIMPLE STEPS

Creating a budget can be overwhelming, but it's really quite simple. It just takes a bit of effort to make sure you know exactly how much you're earning and how much you're spending. Think about it like a game plan for your money, and it's not as intimidating as it seems.

Here are five simple steps to help you get started.

1. **Calculate your income:** This is the first step in creating a budget. You need to know how much money you have coming in every month to make a plan for how to spend it. This includes all sources of income, including your salary or any allowance you may receive and any additional income you might earn through side hustles or investments.

2. **Calculate your spending:** In this step, you'll need to take a close look at how much money you're currently spending. This includes two types of spending:

   • Your regular expenses or needs. These are the things you need to pay for to survive, like a place to live, transportation, communication, and food. These are the essentials that you can't live without.

   • Your discretionary spending or wants, such as dining out, shopping, and entertainment. These expenses are things you choose to spend money on and can live without.

   You'll want to track your spending for at least a month to get a good sense of where your money is going.

3 **Set goals:** Now that you know how much money you have coming in and going out, it's time to set some financial goals. This can be saving for a vacation, buying a car, or a down payment on a house. Whatever your goals, make sure they are specific, measurable, and achievable.

4 **Make a plan:** With your income and spending calculated and your goals set, you can now plan how to reach those goals. This plan should include specific steps for reducing unnecessary expenses, increasing income, and ensuring you're putting enough money into savings to reach your goals.

5 **Track your spending and adjust:** Finally, it's crucial to track your spending and make adjustments as necessary. Review your budget regularly and look for areas to reduce expenses or increase your income. Be flexible and adjust your budget as needed to ensure you're on track to reach your financial goals. Remember, a budget is not a one-time thing; it's an ongoing process.

. . . .

THE 50/30/20 RULE OF BUDGETING

The 50/30/20 rule of budgeting is a simple and effective way to budget your money. It suggests that you divide your after-tax income into three categories:

- 50% for things you need (essential items)

- 30% for things you want (non-essential items)

- 20% for savings or paying off debts

This rule can be helpful because it provides a clear guideline for how to allocate your money, and it's easy to remember.

Let's break it down:

- **50% of your income should be allocated to essential expenses**, like rent, food, and transportation. These are the things you can't avoid that are essential to your survival.

- **30% of your income should be allocated to wants** like eating out, shopping, and going out with friends. These are the non-essential expenses that you can cut back on if you need to save money.

- **20% of your income should be allocated to savings and paying off any debt**. This includes saving for emergencies, investing for the future, and paying off credit card debt.

By following this rule, you can be sure you're allocating enough money for your necessities while allowing yourself some room for fun and saving for the future. It's a simple and effective way to budget your money, ensuring your expenses are in balance.

Activity Time!

Budgeting
Case Study

Background: Jo is a 19-year-old student who is determined to make the most of her time at college.

INCOME

She earns $15/hour at a local part-time job, working Saturdays, earning a total of $450 per month. On top of this, she receives $400 in in financial aid from her college.

EXPENSES

Jo has a number of regular expenses to cover each month. These include rent ($350), food ($150), transport ($100) and online subscriptions ($50). In addition, Jo visits the cinema regularly, spending $50 per month on tickets and snacks. Finally, she has to pay for her textbooks, stationery and other course materials, which come to $100 per month.

How much does Jo spend each month?

Is she spending more than she has coming in?

YES   NO

Which items are wants and which are needs?

Wants:	Needs:

How might Jo reduce her monthly expenditure?

CHAPTER 7. SPENDING –
HOW TO GET MORE FOR LESS!

When it comes to spending your hard-earned money, it's important to be smart about it. Just because you have cash in your pocket doesn't mean you should spend it all at once.

Being smart about your spending is about getting the most for your money and ensuring your dollars go as far as possible. It's about being mindful of your purchases and ensuring you get the best deal. Think of it like a game where the goal is to stretch your money further and make it work harder for you.

In this chapter, we'll look at ways to be a savvy spender and make your money go the extra mile. From finding deals and discounts to learning how to negotiate, we'll cover it all so you can get more for your money.

. . . .

VALUE FOR MONEY

Value can be applied to just about anything, but value for money means getting the best quality or service for the price you pay. It's about making sure that you're not overpaying for something and that you're getting the most bang for your buck.

For example, if you want to buy a new pair of shoes, you might find one that is very cheap but not very durable, meaning it will wear out quickly and you'll have to buy another pair soon. On the other hand, you could find a more expensive pair made with higher-quality materials that will last longer. While the more expensive pair may cost more upfront, it will save you money in the long run because you won't have to replace them as often.

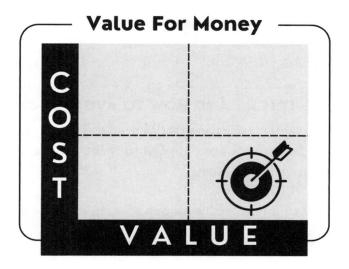

Value For Money

Understanding the concept of value for money can help you make smart financial decisions and ensure you're getting the most for your money.

. . . .

WHAT MAKES SOMETHING GOOD VALUE OR A GREAT DEAL?

When something is considered to be good value or a great deal, it means that it offers a high level of quality or benefit in relation to its cost.

> *For example, if you buy a phone with many features and it functions well, but is not too expensive, it would be considered a great deal. Similarly, if you buy a shirt made of high-quality material that lasts a long time, but is not too expensive compared to other shirts with similar quality, then it would be considered good value for money.*

It's important to note that good value or a great deal can mean different things to different people depending on their needs and preferences. For example, you may find great value in a product that lasts a long time. At the same time, another person may consider a product that is cheaper in price to be a better value.

. . . .

MARKETING TRICKS AND HOW TO AVOID THEM

Be aware of marketing tricks and tactics used to get you to buy something you don't need. Ads are designed to make products attractive, but they can often be misleading.

Here are a few common tactics used in advertising to be aware of:

The 40% Off Savings Illusion

Have you ever walked into a store and seen a sign that says "40% off" and felt like you just found a fantastic deal? While it may seem like you're getting a significant discount, the reality is that the original price may have been marked up to make it seem like you're getting a bigger discount than you actually are. So you have to ask yourself, is the 40% saving really a saving? Is the product even worth the discounted price?

The Limited-Time Offer

A limited-time offer is a marketing strategy businesses use to create a sense of urgency and encourage customers to make a purchase quickly. It usually involves offering a discount or promotion that is only available for a short period, such as 24 hours or one week. The idea behind these offers is to make customers feel a sense of FOMO (the fear of missing out) and get them to make rushed decisions without taking the time to do their research.

The "Bundling" Trick

Also known as "buy one, get one" deals, this strategy encourages you to buy a bundle of products at a discounted price. Bundling items together can save you money, but businesses often use bundling to increase sales of slower-moving products or services by pairing them with more popular items. While the bundle price may be lower than buying each item separately, it's important to consider whether you need all the products or services included in the bundle.

The First Month Free Deal

This is a common tactic used in subscription services. You are offered the first month free. After the free trial period ends, you are automatically charged for subsequent months without realizing it. Although some countries have strict rules about this, it is still a common trick used to get people to sign up for services without fully understanding the terms and conditions or how to cancel.

Celebrity Endorsements

Companies often hire celebrities to promote their products in the hopes that customers will associate their products with the celebrities' positive attributes. Celebrity endorsement may make a product seem more desirable, but it doesn't necessarily mean it is the best value or most suitable choice for you. It's important to remember that they are being paid for their endorsement and may not actually use or believe in the product themselves. Do your own research.

> **DID YOU KNOW?** *The colors used in product packaging and advertising can significantly impact purchasing decisions. Studies have shown that consumers associate different colors with different emotions and personalities. Companies will often choose colors for their products based on the feelings they want to evoke. For example, red is often used to represent excitement and urgency, while blue evokes feelings of calm and trustworthiness.*

HOW TO AVOID THESE MARKETING TRICKS

- **Be an informed consumer**—Take time to research products, compare prices, and read reviews before purchasing.

- **Look for value rather than discounts**—Don't be fooled by offers of huge savings or discounts. Instead, focus on getting the most value for your money.

- **Ignore limited-time offers**—If it's a good deal, it won't disappear overnight. If you're unsure about a product, take your time to make an informed decision.

- **Read the fine print**—Ensure you understand precisely what you're getting and check for additional fees or hidden costs before purchasing anything.

- **Don't be afraid to walk away**—If an offer doesn't seem worth it, don't be scared to walk away. There will always be other deals and opportunities to save money.

By following these steps and understanding how marketing tactics work, you can avoid getting tricked into buying something you don't need or spending more than necessary. Remember, there's more to being smart with your money than just getting discounts—it's about making wise decisions.

. . . .

HOW TO GET MORE FOR LESS

If value for money is about making your money go further, there are some simple tips you can follow to ensure you're getting the most out of your purchases.

Compare Prices

Before making a purchase, research and compare prices from different retailers to ensure you're getting the best deal.

- **Use price comparison websites** to easily compare prices from multiple sellers.

- Consider the total cost of an item, including shipping, taxes, and any additional fees.

Look for Discounts and Coupons

Keep an eye out for discounts, coupons, and promotional deals that can help you save money on your purchases. If you see a box with "Enter Voucher Code" on a checkout page, take the time to search for a discount code or coupon that can be applied to your purchase.

- **Sign up for email newsletters** and alerts from your favorite retailers to receive exclusive discounts and coupons.

- **Check online coupon websites** like RetailMeNot, Coupons. com, and Groupon for deals and discounts.

- **Follow your favorite brands** and stores on social media for special promotions and sales.

- **Add a browser plug-in** like Honey to get the latest discounts.

- Check for student discounts.

- Join loyalty or rewards programs to earn points or cash back on purchases.

Consider Second-Hand or Nearly New

Second-hand or nearly new items often come at a much lower price than brand-new items, meaning you can save money without sacrificing quality.

- **Check online marketplaces** such as Craigslist, Facebook Marketplace, or eBay for gently used items at a lower cost.

- **Visit thrift stores or charity shops** for clothing and household items.

- **Attend garage sales** or markets for unique finds at a discounted price.

- Look for refurbished or reconditioned electronics, which may have been previously used but have been restored to like-new condition.

- Look for open-box or floor-model deals at retail stores, which may have been previously used for display but are still in good condition and sold at a discounted price.

DID YOU KNOW? In addition to the cost-saving benefits, buying second-hand items is also a great way to reduce waste and be more environmentally friendly.

Invest in Quality

"Buy once, buy well"—While it can be tempting to buy cheaper items, investing in products of higher quality can actually save you money in the long run, as they last longer and don't need to be replaced as often.

One way to do this is to consider an item's "cost per use" rather than just the initial price tag. A more expensive item that lasts for years and gets used frequently may be better value than a cheaper item that needs to be replaced often.

For example, you might consider spending more money to buy a pair of shoes that will last longer than a cheaper, lower-quality pair. Instead of buying a new pair of shoes with the lower-quality option every few months, you can invest in higher-quality shoes that may only need to be replaced every couple of years. The cost per use of the higher-quality shoes over the long term is much less than the lower-quality option.

Consider Different Brands and Products

Do your research and compare quality and prices across different brands. Just because a brand is expensive doesn't mean it's the best quality.

So-called "premium brands" often use marketing and advertising tactics to justify their higher prices when you may find the same quality with generic or store-brand products at a lower price.

Buy in Bulk

Buying in bulk is a great way to save money if you know you'll use all the items. Look for stores offering discounts on bulk purchases and buy what you need in larger quantities to get more bang for your buck.

HOW TO REDUCE YOUR MONTHLY SPENDING

If you follow the advice and tips above, you're well on your way to getting more for less. But what about reducing your monthly spending even further? Here are some ways you can do just that.

1. **Cut out subscriptions you don't use:** Think of the streaming services, magazines, or apps you pay for each month. If you're not using them, cancel them. It's like cutting out the fat from your budget.

2. **Make your coffee and lunch:** Instead of buying expensive lattes or takeout, bring your coffee and lunch to school or work. You'll save a lot of money in the long run, and it's like putting money back in your pocket.

3. **Use public transportation or carpool:** Instead of driving or taking an Uber or Lyft everywhere, consider taking the bus or train. Or, if you're going to the same place as a friend, consider carpooling. Not only will you save money on gas and transportation, but you'll also help the environment.

4. **Shop with a list:** Before you go shopping, make a list of what you need and stick to it. Impulse buying can be a budget killer, so think of your list like a game plan for your shopping.

5. **Look for free activities:** Instead of spending money on entertainment, look for free activities like going to a park, visiting a museum, or hiking. It's like finding money in your pocket that you forgot was there.

6. **Do it yourself:** Instead of hiring someone to fix things around the house or care for your car, learn to do it yourself. Search on YouTube for tutorials or ask someone handy to teach you. Over

a lifetime, this can save you a lot of money and be a great way to learn new skills.

> **DID YOU KNOW?** *Saving money can be done without cutting back. One way to save money without reducing spending is by using rewards programs such as cashback sites, loyalty programs, and credit card points. By taking advantage of these opportunities, you can maximize the value of your purchases while also putting some extra savings into your pocket!*

The above are some simple tips to help you reduce your monthly spending, but perhaps the most important thing you can do is to adopt a mindful and money-savvy mindset.

WHAT IS A MONEY-SAVVY MINDSET?

Adopting a money-savvy mindset means being mindful of your spending and finding ways to save money without sacrificing the things you love and enjoy. It's about being creative and resourceful with your money and finding ways to stretch it further. This can include cutting back on unnecessary expenses, looking for deals and discounts, and thinking about the long-term implications of every purchase.

It's not about being cheap or living a minimalist lifestyle but rather about being smart with your money. Simply asking yourself, "Do I really need this?" before buying something can make a huge difference.

Money-Savvy Mindset

Being money-savvy is about being creative and resourceful with your money and finding ways to stretch it further.

Buy

Make

THRIFT

SWAP

Borrow

Use What You Have

For example, instead of buying pre-packaged meals, you could cook your own meals at home with ingredients you buy in bulk. Instead of going out to eat every weekend, you could plan a dinner with friends. Instead of buying new clothes every season, you could learn to sew and make clothes or shop at thrift stores.

By being mindful of your spending and finding creative ways to save money, you can enjoy life without breaking the bank. Start small and look for ways to save money gradually—little steps will eventually add up! It is all about being conscious of your spending habits, so you can enjoy what you love while managing your finances wisely. Good luck!

PART THREE:

BORROWING, DEBT, AND BIG-TICKET ITEM PURCHASES

CHAPTER 8. INTRODUCTION TO BORROWING MONEY AND DEBT

"Too many people spend money they haven't earned to buy things they don't want to impress people they don't like."—*Will Rogers.*

Borrowing and debt are a part of life that allows people to fund their goals and dreams. Without it, many of us couldn't afford things like a home, a car, or a college education. But it's important to understand how borrowing and debt work and how to use them responsibly.

You may think that these topics don't apply to you yet, but the truth is that understanding how borrowing and debt work is important for your financial well-being. As the Will Rogers quote above suggests, going into debt for things you need is one thing, but going into debt for something you don't need can eventually make you poorer.

It's about having a healthy attitude toward debt, minimizing the amount, and knowing the difference between good and bad debt.

In this chapter, we'll be exploring the different types of debt, the pros and cons of borrowing money, and how to make smart financial decisions when taking on debt. You'll learn the difference between good debt and bad debt and how to avoid falling into the trap of taking on too much debt. By the end of this chapter, you'll better understand how to use borrowing and debt responsibly to support your financial goals.

WHAT IS DEBT?

Debt is when you borrow money and agree to pay it back over a period of time, usually with interest (extra money) added on top.

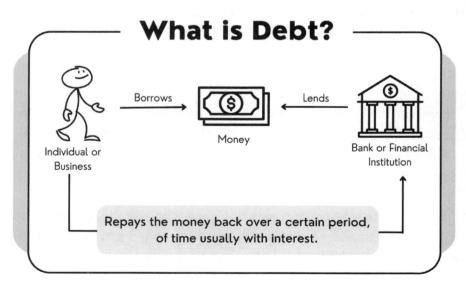

This can be for big things like buying a house or going to college or more minor things like using a credit card. It's a way for individuals or businesses to get the money they need to buy items. Still, it comes with the responsibility of repaying the borrowed amount back with interest over a period of time.

For example, let's say you want to buy a car but don't have enough money saved up. You can borrow money from a bank and agree to pay it back with interest. This means that you'll end up paying more than the original amount you borrowed, but it allows you to get the car you need now instead of waiting until you have enough money saved.

The amount of time to repay the loan, and the interest rate, are determined by the agreement between you and the bank.

DID YOU KNOW? *Debt has been a part of human civilization for thousands of years. In ancient civilizations such as Mesopotamia and Babylon, people used clay tablets to record loans and repayments.*

DEBT VS. CREDIT

It's easy to confuse debt and credit, and the difference between them is subtle.

Debt is the amount of money you owe to someone. It can be a loan, mortgage, credit card balance, or other types of borrowing.

On the other hand, credit is the ability to borrow money or access financing.

Here are two examples:

> **Debt:** *Imagine you borrow $1000 from your parents to buy a new computer. You promise to repay them the $1000 plus interest over a certain period. Your debt is $1000.*

> **Credit:** *If you have a credit card with a $1000 limit, your credit is $1000.*

The difference between debt and credit is that **debt is money you owe to someone** specifically, like a loan from a bank or a friend, while **credit is an agreement with a lender to borrow money up to a specific limit**, like a credit card.

WHO PROVIDES DEBT AND WHY?

Debt is typically provided by financial institutions such as banks, credit unions, and online lenders.

Financial institutions are in the business of making money, and lending is one way they do it. They essentially provide a service—offering individuals and companies money that they need—and the lenders profit from the interest rates paid on each loan.

WHAT ARE INTEREST RATES (OR APR) AND HOW DOES IT WORK?

When you borrow money, you usually have to pay back more than you borrowed because of interest charges and other fees.

The interest rate is the percentage a lender charges on the amount borrowed.

> *For example, if you borrow $1,000 with an interest rate of 5%, you must pay back $1,050 ($1,000 + 5% interest).*

The APR (annual percentage rate) is the total cost of borrowing money over one year, expressed as a percentage. This includes the interest rate charged on the amount borrowed and any additional fees or charges associated with the loan.

> *For example, if you take out a $1,000 loan with an APR of 10%, you would end up paying back $1,100 ($1,000 + 10% interest) over one year.*

The higher the APR, the more expensive it is to borrow money.

Interest rates can vary depending on the type of loan or credit product. They can also be affected by your credit score, the amount you borrow, and the loan term.

A lower interest rate (or APR) is generally better because it means you pay less in interest over the life of the loan.

. . . .

DIFFERENT TYPES OF DEBT

Debt can take many forms. Some common types of debt include secured, unsecured, revolving, nonrevolving, and mortgages. Understanding the differences between these types of debt can help you make informed decisions about borrowing money and managing your finances.

Types of Debt?

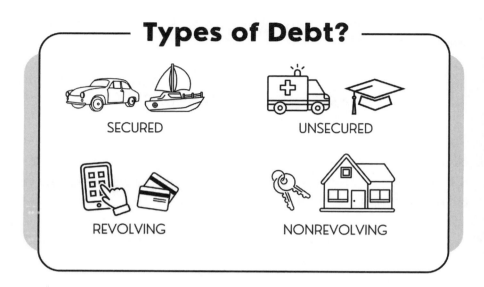

SECURED

UNSECURED

REVOLVING

NONREVOLVING

Secured Debt

This type of debt is backed by something specific (known as "collateral"), such as a car or a house. This means that if you can't repay the borrowed money, the bank or lender can take the item you used as collateral to make up for the money you owe.

> For example, let's say you jump into a brand-new Audi convertible and drive off the dealership lot. You have just taken out a secured debt by taking a car loan. Although you have the keys in your hands and the wind in your hair, you don't own the car. The lender does, and the vehicle you purchased is the collateral. The lender can take the car if you don't repay the loan on time.
>
> Similarly, if you take out a mortgage to purchase a home, the home itself is the collateral and can be taken by the lender if you fail to make the mortgage payments.

This type of debt is often less risky for lenders because they have something they can take if you don't pay them back. As a result, secured debts usually have lower interest rates and more favorable terms than unsecured debt.

Unsecured Debt

This type of debt is not backed by collateral, which means if you can't pay back the money you borrowed, the lender has nothing specific they can take from you to make up for what you owe. Instead, they may take legal action against you or send debt collectors to try and get their money back.

Examples of unsecured debt include personal loans, credit card debt, and medical bills.

These debts are usually riskier for lenders, so they often come with higher interest rates.

Revolving Debt

This type of debt has no set repayment schedule and allows you to borrow money up to a specific limit and then pay it back over time.

The key feature of revolving debt is that the available credit replenishes as you make payments. You can continue borrowing and paying off the balance as long as you stay within your credit limit. A typical example of revolving debt is a credit card. You can use your card to make purchases up to your credit limit and then pay off the balance at your own pace.

> *For example, if you have a credit card with a limit of $10,000 and spend $500, your available credit is reset to $9,500. As you pay off your balance, your available credit increases, and you can continue to borrow and spend up to your limit.*

The danger with this type of debt is that it can lead to many debt and financial difficulties if you don't manage it carefully.

Revolving debt allows you to repeatedly borrow money, which can give the illusion that you have unlimited funds. But if the balance is not paid in full each month, you get charged interest, making it more challenging to pay off the debt. This can lead to a cycle of borrowing and repayment that becomes difficult to break out of.

To avoid this, it's vital to use revolving credit responsibly and **only borrow what you can afford to repay.**

Non-Revolving Debt

This type of debt has a set repayment schedule, with a specific end date for when the loan must be paid back in full. Unlike revolving debt, you cannot continue to borrow once the loan is repaid.

> *For example, if you take out a personal loan to pay for a home renovation project, you will receive a lump sum of money and then make fixed payments until the loan is paid off.*

The advantage of non-revolving debt is that it gives you a clear timeline for when the loan will be paid off and helps you plan your finances more effectively. However, it may also come with higher interest rates compared to revolving debt and may not offer the flexibility to access additional funds if needed.

Mortgages

This type of debt is a loan used to buy a home. You borrow a large sum of money and pay it back over a long time, typically 15–30 years. The property is collateral for the loan, meaning that the bank can take the property to recoup their losses if you don't pay the mortgage.

> *For example, let's say you take out a mortgage of $200,000 to buy a home and agree to make payments over 30 years at a fixed interest rate. Each month, you pay the bank to pay off the principal amount you borrowed ($200,000) and the interest on the loan. As you make payments, the amount you owe decreases. Eventually, after 30 years, you have paid off your mortgage and own the house outright.*

GOOD DEBT VS. BAD DEBT

Not all debt is created equal, and it's essential to understand the difference between good debt and bad debt.

Good Debt vs Bad Debt

What is bad debt?
Bad debt is any type of debt taken on for purchases that do not increase in value or generate income over time.

What is good debt?
Good debt is typically debt that is taken on with the expectation of generating long-term benefits or returns.

Good debt is debt that is taken on for investments that helps you build wealth or generate income in the future.

Some examples of good debt include:

- **A student loan to pay for college education**—This is considered good debt because it can help you get a better job and earn more money in the long run.

- **A mortgage loan**—This is money borrowed from a bank to buy a home. This is also considered good debt, as the price of houses tends to go up in value over time, so the home could eventually be sold for a profit.

Bad debt is any type of debt that does not increase your financial well-being and may harm your financial situation. Some examples of bad debt include:

- **High-interest credit card balances used to purchase non-essential items like clothing**—This is considered bad debt because the purchases are unlikely to increase in value over time.

- **A loan to buy a car that loses value**—This is considered bad debt because the car will likely lose value over time.

The key takeaway is that it's important to understand the difference between good and bad debt and how to use credit responsibly.

Good debt can help you build wealth and gain financial freedom, while bad debt can lead to financial stress and difficulties.

Pros & Cons of Using Debt

PROS

1. Provides funds to make large purchases, such as a home or car.
2. Can be used to invest in a business or education that can lead to higher earning potential in the future.
3. Debt can help manage cash flow during difficult times, such as job loss or medical emergencies.

CONS

1. Too much debt with high interest can make it really hard to keep up with the payments, causing stress and financial problems.
2. Taking on too much debt, can limit your ability to do things you want in the future because you'll have less money available.
3. Not paying your bills on time can hurt your credit score, which makes it harder to borrow money in the future.
4. If you don't pay your bills on time you could lose the item you bought on credit, like a house or car.

WHEN IS DEBT HELPFUL, AND WHEN CAN IT BE A PROBLEM?

Debt can be useful when used to make investments that will ultimately increase your earning potential or improve your overall financial situation, such as taking out a student loan to pay for education or a mortgage loan to buy a house.

However, debt can also be a problem when it is used to purchase unnecessary items or when you cannot make the payments on time, leading to high-interest rates and penalties. This can ultimately cause financial strain and make it challenging to achieve your financial goals.

Additionally, taking on too much debt can make it difficult to handle unexpected financial emergencies.

WHAT SIMPLE STEPS CAN YOU TAKE TO ENSURE YOU'RE USING DEBT RESPONSIBLY AND AVOIDING FINANCIAL TROUBLE?

Some steps you can take include:

- **Avoid taking on** (too much) **debt**.
- Ensure you understand the terms and conditions of any loan or credit before taking it out.
- **Only borrow what you can afford to pay back**.
- Keep track of your payments and due dates, and always pay on time.
- Be mindful of your credit score and maintain a good credit history.
- Be aware of the potential risks and consequences of not being able to make payments.

- Consider seeking advice from a financial professional if you're struggling with debt.

- Be aware of the interest rate, which can significantly affect how much you pay over time.

- Try to pay off debt with the highest interest rate first.

It's important to remember that debt can be a helpful tool when used responsibly, but it can also be very dangerous if not managed properly.

WHAT CAN YOU DO TO GET OUT OF DEBT?

If you're in debt and can't make your payments or have large amounts of debt, there are a few steps you can take.

1 **Speak to the lenders:** See if they can offer you a different repayment plan or if there are any options for consolidating your debt. Most lenders will work with you to find a solution that works for both of you. This could include extending the loan term, lowering the interest rate, or consolidating multiple loans.

2 **Make a budget:** This will help you see where your money is going and where you can make cuts.

3 **Prioritize your debts:** Pay off the debts with the highest interest rates first, as they will cost you more in the long run.

4 **Create a payment plan:** Break down your payments into manageable chunks and make sure you pay at least the minimum amount due each month.

⑤ Look for ways to increase your income: This could be through a part-time job, side hustle, or asking for a raise at your current job.

⑥ Seek help if needed: Several organizations and government programs can help you with debt relief, such as credit counseling services and debt management plans.

⑦ Avoid new debt: Once you're on the road to paying off your existing debts, avoid taking on new debt, which can make it harder to get out of the hole.

Getting out of debt can take time and effort, but you can do it with a plan and determination.

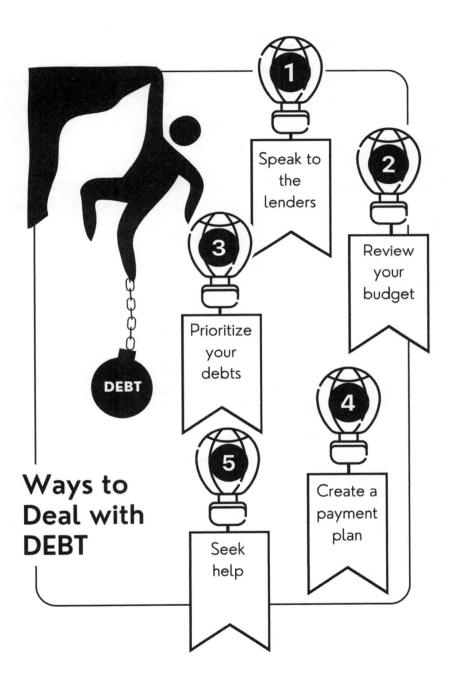

Ways to Deal with DEBT

1. Speak to the lenders
2. Review your budget
3. Prioritize your debts
4. Create a payment plan
5. Seek help

CHAPTER 9. BIG-TICKET ITEM PURCHASES

A big-ticket item usually refers to large, expensive things that cost more than a single paycheck, such as a home, car, expensive furniture, appliances, gadgets, or computers. These purchases often require careful planning and saving to afford them.

As a teen, you may not be considering buying a house or car right now. Still, it's helpful to start thinking about how you can financially prepare for these big purchases in the future.

In this chapter, we'll be talking about the process of saving up for and buying big-ticket items. We'll cover things like setting a budget, saving for a down payment, understanding mortgages, and some of the associated ongoing costs to consider before you make a large purchase.

. . . .

THINGS TO CONSIDER WHEN YOU'RE PLANNING A BIG-TICKET PURCHASE

It can seem daunting when it comes to big-ticket purchases, like buying a house or car. But with a bit of planning and preparation, it doesn't have to be.

Before you start, research the item you are interested in buying. This will help you figure out what's within your budget and what features you can get for your money. You might also find it helpful to seek advice from friends and family about the choices they made. They can probably provide some valuable insights about their experiences and potential pitfalls.

Once you have a good idea of what you're looking for, it's time to start thinking about how you will pay for it.

One option is to save up and buy it outright. This can be a great choice if you have the discipline and financial means to save. But for many people, this isn't an option.

Another option is to borrow money. This can be through a mortgage for a house or a car loan for a vehicle. But it's important to know the costs associated with borrowing, including the interest rate and any fees. It's also important to consider if the loan repayments will be manageable for you in the long term.

It's also essential to consider the ongoing costs of the item, such as property taxes, insurance, and maintenance. This will give you a more accurate picture of the total cost of ownership and help you determine if it's a financially sound decision.

Let's have a look at each of these in turn.

. . . .

BUYING OUTRIGHT VS. BORROWING MONEY

There are two main options when buying big-ticket items: **buying outright** or **borrowing money**.

Buying outright has the benefit of not paying interest on a loan, meaning you'll save money in the long run. It also gives you full ownership of the item and eliminates the risk of defaulting on a loan. However, it also means that you'll need to have the full amount of money saved up, which may not be possible for some people. This might be similar to saving all your allowance for months to buy a new video game console.

On the other hand, borrowing money allows you to purchase the item immediately and spread the cost over some time. This can be helpful if you don't have all the money saved up yet, but it also means you'll have to pay interest on the loan, which can add up over time.

It's important to weigh each option's pros and cons and consider your financial situation before deciding. And always remember to think about the long-term aspects of the purchase, not just the short-term ones.

. . . .

UPFRONT COSTS VS. ONGOING COSTS

When buying big-ticket items, it's vital to consider both upfront costs and ongoing costs.

Upfront costs are the expenses you pay when you first purchase the item, such as a down payment or closing costs. **Ongoing costs are the expenses you pay after the purchase**, such as insurance, maintenance, and repairs.

> *For example, suppose you purchase a car for $20,000. In that case, the upfront costs could include the car's price, a sales tax of 7%, a registration fee of $50, and an extra $1000 for additional features. Ongoing costs might include insurance premiums of $100 per month, regular maintenance costs of $50, and gas expenses of $200 per month.*

When considering a big-ticket purchase, it's crucial to consider both the upfront and ongoing costs and how they will impact your budget over time.

FINANCIAL PLANNING FOR BIG-TICKET ITEMS

A financial plan is a roadmap for saving and managing your money to reach a specific financial goal, such as making a large purchase. Implementing a financial plan for a big purchase involves several steps.

1 **Determine your goal:** Be specific about what you want to purchase and when you want to buy it.

2 **Assess your current financial situation:** Look at your income, expenses, savings, and any existing debts.

3 **Make a budget:** Create a budget that takes into account your goal, current financial situation, and any other financial commitments you have.

4 **Start saving:** Make sure you are setting aside enough money each month to reach your goal.

5 **Look for ways to increase your income:** Consider taking on a part-time job or finding ways to make extra money.

6 **Consider different funding options:** You may be able to buy the item outright, or you may need to borrow money through a loan or mortgage.

7 **Compare costs:** Be aware of any upfront and ongoing costs and ensure you get the best value for your money.

By following these steps, you will be able to create a plan that will help you save up for and purchase your big-ticket item. It's important to remember that saving up for a big purchase will take time, but with a plan, you can reach your goal.

Now let's look at some specific examples.

CHAPTER 10. AN INTRODUCTION TO CAR OWNERSHIP

Owning your first car is an exciting milestone for any young adult. But buying a vehicle is not just about picking out the color and model you like; it is a big financial commitment.

Whether saving up to buy one outright or looking into financing options, it's important to understand the different ways to purchase a car and the ongoing costs of owning one.

In this chapter, we'll explore how the finance side of things work.

HOW TO PAY FOR YOUR FIRST CAR

If you're thinking about buying a car, there are a few things you need to consider.

One of the most important is how you're going to finance it. There are a few options, such as buying outright, financing, and leasing. Each has pros and cons, so it's important to understand what they are before deciding.

- **Buying outright:** If you have enough money, buying a car outright can be a great option. This way, you own the vehicle outright and don't have to worry about making monthly payments. However, this can also be a significant financial burden if you don't have huge savings.

- **Financing:** Another option is to finance a car. This means taking out a loan from a bank or other lender to pay for the vehicle.

This allows you to spread the cost over several years, making it more manageable. However, you'll need to pay interest on the loan, which can add to the cost of the car.

- **Leasing:** A third option is to lease a car. This means paying a monthly fee to use a car for a set period. At the end of the lease, you can buy or return the car. Leasing can be a good option if you don't want to commit to buying a car outright or if you want to drive a newer car. However, you will have mileage and wear-and-tear limits and may not be able to customize the vehicle.

Your First Car

LEASE?

Pros	Cons
-Lower monthly payments	-Must have stable predictable income
-Better warranty protection	-Leases have strict mileage limits
-Get to drive a new car every two to three years	-Likely to pay more overtime
	-Don't own the vehicle

BUY?

Pros	Cons
-Outright ownership	-Higher monthly payments
-Freedom to customize the vehicle	-Post-warranty repair costs
-No end-of-lease charges	-Car value drops over time

ONGOING COSTS

Owning your first car is exciting, but it's important to remember that purchasing a vehicle is just the start. You'll need to budget for many ongoing costs associated with car ownership. Here are a few examples of ongoing costs to keep in mind.

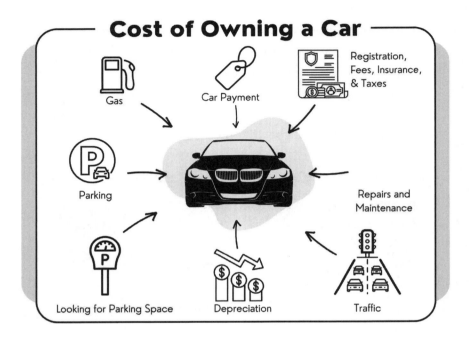

Cost of Owning a Car

Gas

Car Payment

Registration, Fees, Insurance, & Taxes

Parking

Repairs and Maintenance

Looking for Parking Space

Depreciation

Traffic

- **Fuel costs:** You must pay for gasoline, diesel, or electricity to power your car. The cost will depend on the fuel price in your area and how many miles you drive.

- **Insurance:** Most countries require drivers to have car insurance. The insurance cost will depend on factors such as your age, driving record, and the make and model of your car.

- **Maintenance and repairs:** Cars require regular maintenance, such as oil changes, tire rotations, and brake pad replacement. They may also need repairs if something goes wrong. The cost of maintenance and repairs will depend on the car's age, make, model, and how often you drive it.

- **Tires:** Tires need to be changed periodically. The cost will depend on the type of tires and how often you drive.

- **Registration and licensing:** You'll need to pay for registration and licensing for your car, the cost of which can vary depending on where you live.

- **Depreciation:** The value of your car will decrease over time. This is known as depreciation and could affect the resale value of your vehicle, meaning you can't sell it for as much as you paid for it.

- **Parking:** If you don't have a driveway or garage, you may need to pay for parking.

DID YOU KNOW? *According to AAA, the average cost of owning a car in the US is $10,728 per year. This includes car payments, maintenance, fuel, insurance, and depreciation.*

CHAPTER 11. AN INTRODUCTION TO HOME OWNERSHIP

Buying a home is one of the biggest financial decisions you'll ever make. It's a significant investment that can give you a sense of stability and security. But before you start searching for your dream house, it's important to understand how to finance buying a home and what to expect in terms of ongoing costs.

Most people don't have enough money to buy a house outright, so they get a mortgage.

A mortgage is a loan from a bank or other financial institution to buy a home. To get a mortgage, you'll need to put down an initial deposit—usually around 10–20% of the purchase price. This is known as your "down payment." Then, you'll pay back the rest of the loan every month for 15-30 years until it's all paid off.

There are several different types of mortgages available, such as fixed-rate mortgages and adjustable-rate mortgages.

A fixed-rate mortgage is a loan where the interest rate stays the same for the entire duration of the loan. This means your monthly payments will remain the same, no matter what happens in the economy. This can be helpful as it makes budgeting for your mortgage payments easier.

On the other hand, an adjustable-rate mortgage (ARM) has an interest rate that can change over time. This means your monthly payments might increase or decrease depending on the economy. This type of mortgage can be riskier because you don't know how much your payments will be in the future. But it also can have a lower interest rate at the beginning of the loan, which can be helpful for people who cannot initially afford higher payments.

Choosing which type of mortgage is right for you depends on how much money you have saved up, how good your credit score is, and your plans for the future.

> **DID YOU KNOW?** *According to recent data, the average age of first-time homebuyers in the United States is 36.*

HOW MUCH MORTGAGE CAN YOU AFFORD?

When trying to figure out how much mortgage you can afford, there are a few things to keep in mind.

First, mortgage lenders usually look at your income and debts to determine how much you can borrow. They'll typically use a debt-to-income ratio (DTI), which compares your monthly income to your monthly debt payments. This measures how much of your income goes towards paying off your debts, such as credit card payments and car loans. The lower your DTI, the more likely you are to be approved for a mortgage and the more you can borrow.

> *For example, if you earn $5,000 a month and have $1,000 in monthly debt payments, your DTI is 20%. This means that 20% of your income goes towards debt payments. Most lenders typically want your DTI to be at or below 43%.*

The second factor is your gross income, which is your total income before taxes and other deductions. Mortgage lenders usually look at a multiple of your income to determine how much you can borrow.

> *For example, if you make $50,000 a year and the lender uses a multiple of 4, you may be able to borrow up to $200,000.*

The third factor is the down payment, or the money you pay as a deposit. It's usually a percentage of the purchase price—typically at least 5–20%. The bigger the down payment, the smaller the mortgage loan you'll need, which usually results in lower monthly payments.

> *For example, if you're looking to buy a house for $300,000 and can afford to put down 20% or $60,000 as a down payment, you'll need to borrow $240,000. This will lower your monthly mortgage payment.*

A larger down payment can also make getting approved for a mortgage easier and can help you get a better interest rate.

. . . .
HOW LONG ARE MORTGAGES FOR?

When you take out a mortgage to buy a home, the loan is typically spread over 15 to 30 years. This is known as the term of the mortgage. The longer the term, the lower your monthly payments will be, but you'll end up paying more in interest over the life of the loan.

If you decide to move before paying off your mortgage, you have a few options. One is to sell the home and use the money to pay off the remaining balance on the loan. Another option is to refinance the mortgage, which means you get a new loan with a different interest rate or loan term.

You can also consider renting out your home and becoming a landlord. The rent would go towards paying the mortgage and other expenses. Remember that this also brings additional responsibilities, such as finding tenants, managing the property, and dealing with maintenance issues.

ONGOING COSTS OF HOME OWNERSHIP

Owning a home can be an excellent investment, but it comes with ongoing costs. These include:

- **Property taxes**—You'll have to pay taxes on your property every year. The amount you pay depends on how much your home is worth and the tax rate where you live.

- **Homeowners insurance**—This kind of insurance protects your home and belongings if something terrible happens, like a natural disaster or theft. Usually, banks require you to have it if you have a mortgage.

- **Maintenance and repairs**—As a homeowner, it's up to you to ensure your house stays in good condition. This means fixing things that break like leaky pipes, painting walls, or replacing the roof when it gets old.

- **Utilities**—When you own a house, you pay for things like electricity, gas, water, and the internet. Make sure to budget for these expenses so you don't get surprised by high bills!

It's essential to keep these ongoing costs in mind when you're budgeting for a home purchase. Setting aside money each month for unexpected repairs is also a good idea. After all, you never know what's going to happen.

PART FOUR:

YOUR WAY TO WEALTH

CHAPTER 12. SAVING–YOUR RAINY DAY FUND

Saving money is integral to learning to be responsible with your finances, regardless of age. It's like building a fortress around your future—the more you save, the stronger and more secure it will be!

Saving can take many forms from setting aside a certain amount each month to investing in stocks or bonds. It's all about having the discipline to put money away for a rainy day and not spending it on something you don't need right now.

> **DID YOU KNOW?** *The concept of "saving for a rainy day" originated in India. It was common practice to set aside grains during times of plenty to use during drought or famine.*

SAVING VS. INVESTING

Saving and investing are ways to grow your money, but they work in different ways.

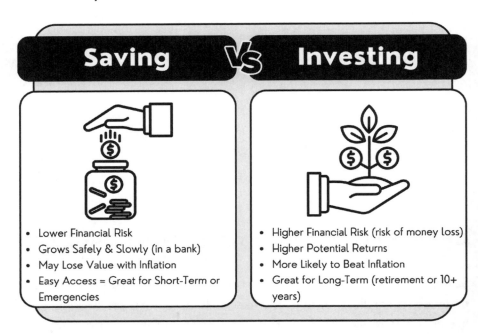

Saving VS Investing

- Lower Financial Risk
- Grows Safely & Slowly (in a bank)
- May Lose Value with Inflation
- Easy Access = Great for Short-Term or Emergencies

- Higher Financial Risk (risk of money loss)
- Higher Potential Returns
- More Likely to Beat Inflation
- Great for Long-Term (retirement or 10+ years)

Saving money is when you put aside a portion of your income for future use, usually into a savings account at a bank. You're setting it aside for a specific goal or rainy day. This money will grow slowly, and it's generally considered a lower-risk option. In addition, the money is easily accessible when you need it. *For example, you might save money for a car down payment or emergency fund.*

Investing, on the other hand, is like planting a seed in the ground. When you invest, you're putting your money into something like stocks, bonds, or real estate with the expectation that it will grow in value over time. It's generally considered a higher-risk option but can also create greater returns.

While saving helps you to put money aside for short-term goals and emergencies, investing is about growing your money over the long term—but you need to be comfortable with the higher risk involved.

· ·

WHY IT PAYS TO START SAVING YOUNG

It's never too early to start thinking about saving. The earlier you start, the better—for several reasons.

The Power of Compound Interest

The earlier you start saving, the more time your money has to grow. This is because of the power of compound interest.

Compound interest is where the interest earned is added to the original amount of money. Then future interest is earned on top of that. This means that the longer you save your money, the more interest it will make, and the more your money will grow.

> *Imagine you put $100 into a savings account that earns 10% interest per year. After one year, you would have $110. But if you left that $110 in the account for another year, it would earn 10% interest again, bringing the total to $121. The longer you leave your money in the account, the more it will grow.*

Here's another example:

> Let's say two individuals, Jane and Mike, want to save for retirement.
> Jane starts saving at age 21 and manages to save a total of $24,000
> by the time she is 41, at which point she stops saving. Mike doesn't
> start saving until age 47 and manages to save $24,000 until he
> retires at 67.
>
> Assuming an annual interest rate of 8%, Jane's investment of $24,000
> will have grown to $471,358 by the time she retires at 67.
>
> On the other hand, Mike started later, so his investment of $24,000
> has had less time to grow and is only worth $59,295 by the time he
> retires at 67.

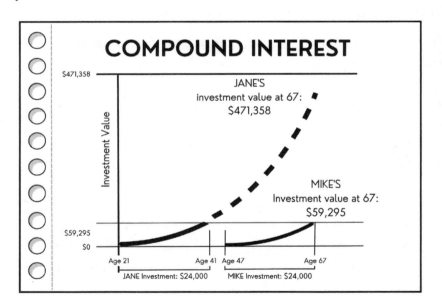

Time is one of the most significant advantages when saving and investing. The longer your money has to compound, the more it can grow over time—even with a small amount of savings each month!

Starting Young Helps Develop Good Financial Habits

Another reason why it pays to start saving young is that it helps you develop good financial habits. The more you save and budget your money, the more you will understand how to make your money work for you. It's like learning a new skill—the more you practice, the better you get.

> *For example, if you start saving $50 a month from age 16, you will have $3,600 saved by the time you are 21 ($50 x 12 months x 6 years). That's a lot of money that could be used for a down payment on a car or an emergency fund.*

Starting Young Prepares You for Unexpected Events

Additionally, if you start saving young, you'll be more prepared for unexpected expenses or big life events like college, buying a house, or starting a family. It's like planning a trip—the more you plan, the better prepared you are.

Saving may not be the most exciting thing, but it's an important step toward financial independence and security. It will give you the freedom to make choices and pursue opportunities that might otherwise be out of reach.

HOW TO SAVE MONEY

As we have explored above, starting to save money at a young age is essential—but how do you actually do it? Here are a few tips:

1. Make Saving a Habit

First, just focus on making saving a habit and gradually increase your savings once it becomes comfortable. Don't feel like you have to jump in with enormous contributions right away. Setting aside just $5 or $10 each month will help get you started on the right track.

2. Have Goals and Track Your Progress

Having clear goals will help you stay motivated when it comes to saving. Making sure you track your progress along the way will make those goals seem more achievable and keep you on track toward reaching them.

> *For example, you might set a goal of saving $1,000 for college by the time you turn 18. You can then break this down into smaller goals and track your progress each month to see how much closer you are to achieving it.*

3. Have Multiple Accounts

Having multiple savings accounts can help you better manage your money. You could have a short-term savings account to save for things like holidays and a long-term savings account to save for things like college or buying your first car. You can usually set up multiple savings accounts at your bank, but you may want to shop around for the highest interest rates.

4. Automate Your Savings

Setting up an automatic transfer from your primary checking account into your savings accounts each month is a great way to ensure you don't forget about putting money into savings. Automating your savings also helps you save more because it removes the temptation of spending that money before it goes into your savings account.

5. Look for Ways to Earn Extra Money

Look for part-time jobs or freelance work that you can do during your free time, or even consider starting your own small business. The extra income can go straight into your savings account, helping you reach your goals faster.

6. Look for Deals and Discounts

Saving money doesn't always mean putting money away. It can also mean finding ways to cut back on your spending.

When you're shopping for anything, always be on the lookout for deals and discounts. By taking advantage of sales and coupons, you can save money on your purchases and put more into your savings account. You can also look into free trials, samples, and freebies or buy used items.

> **DID YOU KNOW?** Small, everyday expenses can add up to significant savings over time. For example, skipping a $5 latte every workday for a year would save you $1,300!

7. Learn to Budget and Prioritize Expenses

Creating a budget will help you understand how much money you have coming in and going out each month. Prioritizing your expenses and cutting back on unnecessary spending can free up more money for your savings.

> *For example, instead of buying a new video game every month, you could save that money towards a bigger purchase, like a laptop or a new bike.*

8. Start Small and Grow Your Savings

Remember, starting small is better than not starting at all. Even if you can only save a little bit each month, that's better than nothing. Over time, as you get used to saving and building the habit, you can gradually increase the amount you save each month.

By having a plan and sticking to it, you can start building a healthy financial future from a young age with just small steps each day.

- -

SIMPLE SAVINGS METHODS

Now that you have a good idea of how to save money, let's explore some of the methods to put that into practice.

The Envelope Method

The envelope system is a simple method of budgeting that involves physically dividing your cash into different envelopes labeled with various expenses, such as "groceries" or "entertainment." When the money in an envelope runs out, you know you need to stop spending on that category for the rest of the month.

This system can also be adapted for online banking and budgeting apps. Instead of using physical envelopes, you would create virtual "envelopes" or categories within the app and assign a certain amount of money to each.

> *For example, you could set a budget for "shopping" and "eating out" and transfer the appropriate amount into those categories at the beginning of each month. When the funds in a category run low, it serves as a reminder to cut back on spending in that area.*

The Save First Method

The Save First Method is another simple savings method that can help you build a habit of saving. The basic idea behind this method is to save a certain percentage of your income **before** spending it on other things. This can be a set percentage, such as 10% or 20%, or a flexible percentage based on your income and expenses.

Even though you may not yet have a full-time job, you can still apply this method to your allowance or part-time job income.

> *For example, let's say you get a part-time job and earn $500 a month. Under the 50/30/20 system, you would allocate $250 for necessities like housing, food, and transportation, $150 for wants like shopping, entertainment, and dining out, and $100 for savings.*

Another way to apply the save first method is to set up an automatic transfer from your main checking account into your savings accounts each month. This way, your savings will be taken care of before you even have a chance to spend it.

It's important to note that the Save First Method is adaptable, and you can adjust the percentages to suit your financial situation. The most important thing is to prioritize saving and build it into your regular budget.

These strategies are great for getting into the habit of saving money and ensuring that you have a healthy financial future. Whether setting up multiple savings accounts, automating your transfers, or putting aside some cash as soon as you get it, there are many easy ways to start saving today!

. . . .

SAVINGS AND TAX

This is not a book about taxes, but it's helpful to understand tax regarding savings.

When you save money, sometimes the government will take a small percentage of that money in taxes. This is called "tax on savings." It's similar to paying taxes on the money you earn from a job.

There are different types of savings accounts, some of which are "tax-efficient," meaning that you don't have to pay as much tax on the money you save in them. In fact, some savings accounts are called "tax-free savings accounts" because you don't have to pay any tax on the interest you earn from them.

It's important to remember that taxes can be complex and differ by country. You should talk to a tax professional or financial advisor if you have any tax questions or if are unsure how taxes work with your savings and investments.

The 100 Envelope Challenge

STEP 1	Get 100 Envelopes
STEP 2	On each envelope, write a number from 1-100.
STEP 3	Each day, pick an envelope at random. Whatever number is on the envelope, put that amount of money inside it.
STEP 4	Repeat step 3 everyday until you have filled all of the envelopes.
STEP 5	Congrats! If you'd successfully completed the challenge, you'll have saved $5,050!

CHAPTER 13. INVESTING – BUILDING WEALTH

Investing can seem mysterious and daunting, but it's a lot simpler than it appears.

Imagine your money is like a seed you plant in fertile soil. That seed can grow into a healthy and strong tree with the right amount of water, sunshine, and care.

Investing works in a similar way! Putting your money into different types of high-quality investments can help it grow and become more valuable over time.

Like a garden, you can make many different types of investments, each with its own risk level and potential reward. Some investments, like stocks or businesses, have the potential to snowball, but they also come with a higher level of risk.

Other investments, like bonds or savings accounts, offer a more stable and reliable return but with lower growth potential. When investing, the key is to find the right balance between risk and reward to help your money grow in a way that works best for you.

In this chapter, we'll be exploring the world of investing. We'll look at the different types of investments available to grow your money. We'll review the pros and cons of each and help you understand the risk vs. reward aspect of investing. Finally, we'll talk about the importance of having a long-term horizon when it comes to investing and the difference between short-term and long-term investments.

But first up, what exactly is investing?

Investing is putting your money into something with the hope of making more money in the future.

When you invest your money, you are buying a piece of something, like a company (stocks), real estate (property), or a loan to a company or government (bonds). These investments can generate income or grow in value so you can sell them later for a profit.

The idea behind investing is to put your money to work, instead of letting it sit in a savings account. But while you can make money by investing, you can also lose money if the investment doesn't perform well. This is why educating yourself and understanding the different types of investments and their associated risks is crucial.

. . . .

DIFFERENT TYPES OF INVESTMENTS

When you start to build out your financial portfolio, there are many different types of investments available to you. Each comes with pros, cons, risks, rewards, and time horizon. Let's have a look at some of them:

Stocks

When you buy stocks, you essentially buy a small piece of ownership in a company. *For example, if a company has 100 shares and you buy one share, you own 1% of that company.* Companies sell shares of their stock on the stock market to raise money and to give people a chance to own a piece of the company.

When you buy a share of stock, you have the potential to make money in two ways.

1 **Capital appreciation:** If the company does well and its stock price increases, you can sell your shares for a profit.

2 **Dividends:** If the company is profitable, you may also receive a portion of the company's profits in the form of dividends, which are payments made to shareholders.

However, there is also a risk involved with buying stocks. **If the company does poorly, its stock price might decrease, and you could lose money.** That's why it's essential to research and make informed decisions before buying stocks.

Pros: High potential for growth and an excellent way to participate in a company's growth.

Cons: The stock market can go up and down. There's always the risk that a company could go bankrupt, and your investment could be lost.

Time horizon: Long-term (five years or more).

> **DID YOU KNOW?** The world's first stock market was established in Amsterdam in 1602 by the Dutch East India Company. The company issued shares to investors, making it one of the earliest examples of a publicly traded company.

Bonds

When you purchase a bond, you essentially lend funds to a company or government. In return, they promise to pay you back the amount you lent, plus interest, over an agreed-upon time. The company or government uses your money to finance its operations or pay for big projects.

Think of buying a bond like lending your friend some money. They promise to pay you back the amount you lent, plus a little extra for letting them use your money. Just like with your friend, when you buy a bond, there's a risk that the company or government won't be able to pay you back. In general, however, bonds are considered less risky than stocks.

When the bond reaches the end of its term, the company or government will pay you back the amount you lent. The interest you receive from a bond is usually paid to you in regular payments. The interest you receive is based on the interest rate agreed upon when you bought the bond.

> *For example, let's say you purchased a $1,000, 10-year bond with a 5% annual interest rate. In this case, you would receive $50 per year in interest payments until the bond reaches maturity in 10 years. At that point, you would receive your original $1,000 investment back.*

Generally, bonds can be a good investment choice for people looking for a relatively stable and predictable source of income. However, it's important to remember that bond prices can still go down, and there's always some risk involved.

Pros: Bonds are generally considered a lower-risk investment than stocks and can provide a steady income stream.

Cons: The returns on bonds are usually lower than those of stocks, and there's a risk that the borrower could default on the loan.

Time horizon: Medium-term (1 to 10 years).

Different Types of Investments

Investment Type	Description	Risk	Reward
Stocks	Stocks are a way to own a small piece of a company and potentially make money if the company does well.	High	High
Bonds	Bonds are investment options where your money is invested with a government or company, and they promise to pay you back with interest.	Low	Low
Funds	Funds are a way to invest money in a group of companies or assets, sometimes managed by professionals or passively following an index.	Medium	Medium
Property	Real estate investing refers to buying and owning property, such as apartments, with the goal of generating income or appreciation.	Depends on Portfolio	High
Alt. Assets	Alternative assets are investments in assets other than stocks, bonds, and real estate. These include metals, energy, & even cryptocurrency.	High	?

Funds

A fund is a type of investment that pools money from many different investors to buy a variety of different assets, such as stocks, bonds, or real estate. When you invest in a fund, you own a small piece of the entire portfolio of assets instead of just one individual stock or bond. This can be an excellent way to diversify your investments, spreading your money across different types of assets to reduce risk.

There are two main types of funds: actively managed funds and passively managed funds.

1. Actively Managed Funds

Actively managed funds are managed by a professional fund manager who makes investment decisions on behalf of the fund's investors based on their judgment and expertise. The fund manager selects the assets to include in the fund and continually monitors the portfolio's performance to make necessary changes.

Pros: Potential for higher returns, as the fund manager uses their expertise and research to make investment decisions on behalf of the fund's investors. Additionally, actively managed funds can be more flexible. The fund manager can adjust the investments in response to market conditions.

Cons: Higher fees, as the fund manager's salary and research expenses are reflected in the fund's expense ratio. Additionally, actively managed funds may underperform passive funds over the long term due to the higher fees and the difficulty of consistently outperforming the market.

Time horizon: Can be short-term or long-term, depending on the fund manager.

2. Passively Managed Funds

Passively managed funds, also known as index funds or ETFs, track a specific market index, sector, or region. The idea behind these funds is to provide investors with a low-cost, diversified way to invest in the stock market. Instead of trying to beat the market through active stock picking and frequent trading, passively managed funds simply aim to match the performance of the underlying index.

> *For example, an S&P 500 index fund invests in all 500 companies included in the S&P 500, in proportion to their weighting in the index. If the S&P 500 index goes up, the fund is also expected to increase. Similarly, if the S&P 500 index goes down, the fund would be expected to go down.*

Passively managed funds have become increasingly popular in recent years due to their lower costs and simplicity than actively managed funds. They are often considered a good option for long-term investment, especially for novice investors who are just starting to build their portfolios.

Pros: Passive funds are easy to buy and sell, provide diversification, and have low fees.

Cons: The performance of ETFs and index funds are tied to the underlying assets, so there's always a risk that those assets could decline in value.

Time horizon: Can be short-term or long-term, depending on the fund.

> **DID YOU KNOW?** *Studies have shown that passive funds tend to outperform managed funds over the long term due to lower fees and expenses.*

Property

Real estate investing refers to buying and owning property, such as apartments, office buildings, and retail spaces, to generate income or sell and profit if the price increases. Like funds, real estate investing allows you to diversify your investments and spread your money across different assets.

One way to invest in real estate is to directly buy a property, such as a rental or vacation home. Another way is to invest in a real estate investment trust (REIT), a type of fund that invests in income-generating properties. REITs can be publicly traded, like stocks, or privately held.

The main advantage of real estate investing is the potential for steady income from rent and the potential for an increase in the value of the property over time.

Pros: Property has the potential to provide a stable source of income and can go up in value over time.

Cons: Property investments can be expensive and require much maintenance. In addition, there's always the risk that property prices could fall. They can also be difficult to sell. Additionally, vacant rental properties can soon wipe out any potential profits.

Time horizon: Long-term (five years or more).

Businesses

When you invest in a small business, you essentially become a part owner of the company and share in its potential profits and losses. You can invest in a small business by putting money into a startup, buying into an established business, or even setting up your own business.

Investing in a startup can be risky, as many fail within the first few years of operation. However, if you believe in the business idea and the people behind it, you could potentially reap substantial rewards if the business is booming.

Buying into an established business can offer a lower-risk option, as the company has already proven its ability to survive and generate profits.

However, the potential for reward may also be lower, as the company may already be close to its growth potential.

Starting your own business can also be a form of investing, as you put your time, energy, and money into building a company from the ground up. This can be a high-risk, high-reward option, as you have complete control over the success or failure of the business.

Pros: The potential for high returns, being your own boss, and having control over your investment.

Cons: Business investments can be risky, and there's always the possibility that the business could fail.

Time horizon: Long-term (five years or more).

> **DID YOU KNOW?** *Steve Jobs (the co-founder of Apple) paid his first employees at Apple with stock options, which meant they could purchase Apple shares at a discounted price. Those early employees, including a secretary and a graphic designer, did well to accept his offer, becoming millionaires when the company went public years later.*

Alternative Assets

Alternative asset investing refers to investments in assets other than stocks, bonds, and real estate. These include commodities such as precious metals or energy, hedge funds, private equity, and cryptocurrency.

When you invest in alternative assets, you own a small piece of the asset, similar to investing in a stock or bond. The asset's value can fluctuate based on market conditions and the specific asset's performance.

Investing in alternative assets can be a way to diversify your investments, reducing risk by spreading your money across different types of assets. However, alternative assets can also be riskier and more volatile than traditional investments, and there is often a lack of information available about the performance and prospects of these investments.

Cryptocurrency, for example, is a relatively new and rapidly evolving asset class that has seen significant price swings in recent years. Investing in cryptocurrency can offer the potential for high returns but also involves a high degree of risk and uncertainty.

When considering alternative asset investments, it's essential to understand the potential risks and rewards, as well as your personal investment goals and risk tolerance. It is also helpful to consult a financial advisor to determine whether alternative assets are appropriate for your investment portfolio.

Pros: Alternative asset investing allows investors to invest in unique and innovative assets that offer diversification with the potential for higher returns.

Cons: Higher risk than traditional investments due to lack of regulation, information, and stability in some alternative markets. Additionally, it can be difficult to accurately value and understand these assets.

Time horizon: Short-term to medium-term (one to five years).

One approach to potentially reduce risk is to create a diversified portfolio that includes a mix of different types of investments to spread your investments across different assets. This helps to minimize the impact of any losses and may provide a better chance of generating a positive return over the long term.

. . . .

THE IMPORTANCE OF DIVERSIFICATION

Diversification is a key principle of investing that involves spreading your money across various assets to reduce risk.

Investing in a diverse range of assets can help minimize the impact of any one investment that may not perform well. When one investment performs poorly, if you are well diversified, another investment will likely perform better, which helps to balance out your overall returns.

> *For example, imagine an investor with all their money invested in just one stock. If that stock performs badly, their entire portfolio will drop in value. On the other hand, the impact might be reduced if that same investor had diversified their investments across a range of stocks, bonds, real estate, and alternative assets.*

Diversification can also help reduce your portfolio's overall volatility, which can be beneficial in uncertain market conditions. Investing in various assets helps ensure that you are not overexposed to any one market or sector, which helps minimize the risk of loss.

. . . .

VOLATILITY AND HAVING A LONG-TERM HORIZON

Volatility refers to the ups and downs in the value of an investment over time. In other words, it's a measure of how much the price of an investment fluctuates. Some investments, such as stocks, can be very volatile and experience big swings in price. In contrast, others, such as bonds, tend to be less volatile.

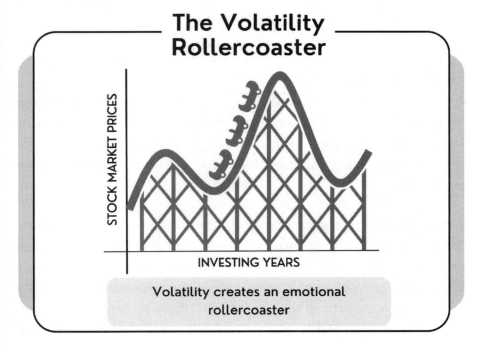

The Volatility Rollercoaster

STOCK MARKET PRICES

INVESTING YEARS

Volatility creates an emotional rollercoaster

A long-term approach to investing can help you weather the ups and downs of volatility. By investing long-term, you can give your investments time to grow and recover from any short-term losses. This is why many investors choose to invest in a diversified portfolio of assets, with a mix of stocks, bonds, and other investments, and hold onto their investments for several years or even decades.

> *For example, if you invested $10,000 in the S&P 500 index at the end of 1999, you would have seen the value of your investment fall dramatically during the crash in 2000 and 2001. However, if you had held onto your investment and not sold, your investment would have grown to more than $40,000 by the end of 2019, despite the ups and downs in the market along the way.*

This demonstrates the power of having a long-term perspective and not being scared off by short-term drops.

UNDERSTANDING RISK

Risk tolerance refers to an individual's willingness and ability to accept the possibility of losses in exchange for the potential for higher returns when investing. It's important because it helps determine what types of investments suit a particular individual and what level of risk they can handle.

Everyone's risk tolerance is different, and it's influenced by several factors, including age, financial situation, investment experience, and personal goals. Some people are comfortable taking on high levels of risk and are willing to tolerate short-term losses to potentially achieve higher returns in the long term. Others prefer more conservative investments, with a lower risk of loss but also a lower potential for growth.

> *For example, a young person with a long time horizon and a high-risk tolerance might be comfortable investing a significant portion of their*

savings into a portfolio of high-risk, high-reward assets, such as stocks and real estate. In contrast, an older person close to retirement with a lower risk tolerance might prefer a more balanced portfolio with a mix of stocks and bonds and cash and other low-risk assets.

WHY IT PAYS TO START EARLY

We have already looked at compounding interest in the previous chapter, but it is so important that it's worth revisiting.

Compounding is the process by which an investment earns returns, not just on the original investment but also on the returns earned over time. It is a powerful way to grow wealth over the long term.

The importance of starting early cannot be overstated. The earlier you start investing, the more time you have for your investment to compound and grow.

For example, if, at 20 years of age, you were to invest $100 per month into a stock portfolio that earns an average of 7% per year, after 40 years, you would have invested a total of $48,000, but your portfolio would be worth nearly $240,000.

Now consider if you wait until you are 40 to start investing, but you save $200/month. After 20 years, despite investing the same amount of money ($48,000), your total investments be worth just under $100,000.

That's a huge difference—and that's the power of compounding. The bottom line is that starting early and taking advantage of the power of compounding can significantly impact your financial future.

It is never too early to start thinking about your investments and how you can grow your wealth over time.

. . . .

GET STARTED IN SIX SIMPLE STEPS:

Starting to invest can seem overwhelming, but it can be broken down into six simple steps. By following these steps, you can start investing and building wealth over time.

Step 1: Determine Your Investment Goals

The first step to investing is to determine your investment goals. What do you want to achieve through investing? Your investment goals will guide your decision-making process and help you choose the right investments.

> *For example, let's say you are a 10th grader who wants to save up for college. Your investment goal might be to have enough money to cover tuition and fees by the time you start college. In this case, you might focus on investments designed to grow your money over the medium term, such as stocks or funds.*
>
> *As another example, let's say you are saving for a short-term goal, like a trip to Europe. Your investment goal might be to have enough money saved up to pay for your trip in the next year. In this case, you might focus on less volatile investments that are less likely to lose value, such as bonds or a high-interest savings account.*

It's important to determine your investment goals before you start investing because it will help you make decisions that align with your financial goals and what you want to achieve.

Step 2: Assess Your Risk Tolerance

The second step is to assess your risk tolerance. How comfortable are you with the idea of losing money? Some people are willing to take on more risk to pursue higher returns, while others prefer a more conservative approach. Understanding your risk tolerance will help you choose investments that align with your comfort level.

> *For example, if you have a low-risk tolerance, you may prefer investments that are more stable and predictable, such as bonds or index funds. On the other hand, if you have a higher risk tolerance, you may be more interested in investments with the potential for higher returns but also carry a greater risk, such as stocks or real estate.*

Here are a few ways to assess your risk tolerance.

- **Consider your personal financial situation:** If you have a large emergency fund, a stable income, and no immediate need for your investment capital, you may be able to tolerate more risk. On the other hand, if you have a lot of debt, a single income, and an immediate need for the money you're investing, you may prefer to be more conservative.

- **Think about your personality:** Some people are naturally more risk averse, while others are comfortable taking on more risk. Consider your personal comfort level with risk when making investment decisions.

- **Use online tools:** There are many online tools available to help you determine your risk tolerance. They are not perfect, but they can give you a good idea of your risk tolerance.

Step 3: Educate Yourself on the Different Types of Investments

The third step is to educate yourself on the different types of investments available. This can include stocks, bonds, mutual funds, exchange-traded funds (ETFs), real estate, and more. Take the time to understand the risks and rewards associated with each type of investment and consider which types may align with your goals and risk tolerance.

> **DID YOU KNOW?** *A $100 investment in the S&P500 in 1990 was worth $2,148 in 2022. That's a 2,048% increase or a 9.79% yearly return.*

Step 4: Open a Brokerage Account

The fourth step is to open a brokerage account. This is an account that allows you to buy and sell investments. There are various kinds of brokerage accounts available, including conventional brokerage accounts, robo-advisory services, and self-managed accounts.

Here are some things to consider when choosing a brokerage.

- **Fees:** Some brokerages charge fees for trading or for maintaining your account. Be sure to compare the fees charged by different brokerages and choose one that suits your budget. However, remember that cheaper doesn't always equal better.

- **Ease of use:** Consider how easy it is to use the brokerage's website or mobile app. You may want to look for a brokerage that offers helpful educational resources and tools to help you make informed investment decisions.

- **Investment options:** Make sure the brokerage offers the type of investments you're interested in, such as stocks, bonds, mutual funds, etc.

- **Customer service:** Look for a brokerage with good customer service so you can get help and support when you need it.

Once you've chosen a brokerage, you must provide personal and financial information to open an account. You'll also need to link the account to a bank account so that you can deposit money into the account and make trades.

Step 5: Start Investing

Once you've completed the first four steps of your investment journey, it's finally time to start investing! This is where you put your knowledge and preparation into action and start building your portfolio.

Depending on your investment goals and risk tolerance, you can do this in a few different ways.

Here are some options to consider.

- **Start small:** Starting small can help you gain confidence and experience in investing. It can also help you avoid making big mistakes that could impact your financial situation.

- **Invest in mutual funds or exchange-traded funds (ETFs):** If you're looking for a more hands-off approach, you can invest in mutual funds or ETFs. These are pools of investments managed by professional fund managers, providing a level of diversification that can help reduce risk.

- **Start with a robo-advisor:** If you're new to investing and want a low-cost, automated option, consider starting with a robo-advisor.

These services use algorithms to manage your investments for you. They can be a great way to get started if you're not yet comfortable making investment decisions on your own.

- **Buy individual stocks or bonds:** Once you feel confident in choosing specific assets, you can purchase individual stocks or bonds directly through your brokerage account. This can give you more control over your investments, but it also comes with greater risk and requires more research and monitoring.

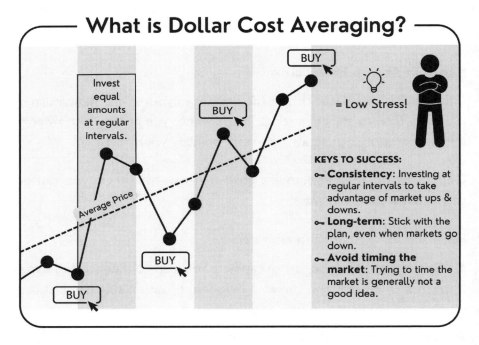

What is Dollar Cost Averaging?

Invest equal amounts at regular intervals.

Average Price

BUY

BUY

BUY

BUY

= Low Stress!

KEYS TO SUCCESS:
- **Consistency**: Investing at regular intervals to take advantage of market ups & downs.
- **Long-term**: Stick with the plan, even when markets go down.
- **Avoid timing the market**: Trying to time the market is generally not a good idea.

- **Consider dollar-cost averaging:** This is a strategy where you regularly invest a fixed amount of money over a long period of time rather than investing a lump sum all at once. This can help reduce the risk of investing in volatile markets, as you buy more units when prices are low and fewer units when prices are high.

Step 6: Automate Your Investing

Once you've started investing, you might consider automating your investments. Automating your investing involves setting up a regular schedule for investing a set amount of money into your brokerage account. This can be done on a monthly, bi-monthly, or quarterly basis. The idea behind automating your investments is to take the emotion out of investing and make it a habit. By investing small amounts of money regularly, you can reduce the impact of market volatility and benefit from the power of compounding over time.

Automating your investments is easy and can be done through your brokerage account. You can specify the amount you want to invest, the frequency of your investment, and the investment vehicle you want your money to go into. This can help you stay disciplined in your investing and ensure that you are consistently putting money towards your financial goals.

Regardless of your chosen approach, the key is to start investing early and to remain disciplined about your investment plan. Remember that investing is a long-term game. It's important to stick to your goals and stay the course, even during market ups and downs.

In conclusion, these six steps will help you get started with investing. Investing can be a powerful tool for building wealth over time, but it's essential to be patient and disciplined in your approach.

PART FIVE:

THE FUTURE OF MONEY

Money has come a long way since the days of bartering goods and services. Although we still have cash, checks, and credit cards, we increasingly rely on digital payment forms.

In recent years, there has been a growing trend towards a cashless society, with people using apps on their smartphones or other digital devices to pay for goods and services. This shift is driven mainly by advances in technology and the growing popularity of online and mobile banking.

In this chapter, we will explore how money is changing and what it means for young people like you. We will look at how our relationship with money is becoming more digital as we move from land-based banking to the internet, and then to app-based banking.

We will also examine the potential consequences of this shift as money becomes more like digits on a screen than something you hold in your hand. With instant gratification just a tap away, it's helpful to understand how this can impact spending habits and financial well-being.

CHAPTER 14. FROM CASH TO CASHLESS

In recent years, society has been moving towards a cashless economy.

In this new cashless economy we are more and more reliant on digital forms of payment such as credit cards, debit cards, and mobile payment apps like Apple Pay and Venmo. This shift towards a cashless society has been driven by technological advancements and the convenience of digital payments for consumers and businesses.

> **DID YOU KNOW?** *The move to a cashless society could lead to the extinction of coins and banknotes? This means that future generations might not even know what physical money looks like!*

. . . .

WHAT THIS MEANS FOR YOU

On the positive side, shifting towards a cashless society offers many conveniences.

With electronic payment methods like debit and credit cards, mobile wallets, and online banking, it's easier to make purchases and keep track of your spending with mobile banking apps. Transactions can be processed quickly and securely, and you don't need to carry cash. In addition, cashless transactions are often more convenient and faster than traditional methods, as you can make purchases with just a tap of your phone or a click of a button.

However, there are also some potential downsides. For one, relying solely on digital payments may make you more vulnerable to identity theft and fraud. Additionally, not having readily available cash can make it harder to stick to a budget, as you may be more likely to overspend when using electronic payment methods.

> *For example, overspending can be easier when you don't physically see the money leaving your pocket or bank account.*

When money becomes just digits on a screen, there can be a disconnect between the value of your spending and the physical items you're buying. This is because you no longer have a tangible representation of your spending money, like physical cash or coins. When you can't physically see the money leaving your account, losing track of your spending and overspending can be easier. This is particularly true in a world of instant gratification, where you can make purchases with a tap on a screen or a swipe of your phone.

. . . .

INSTANT GRATIFICATION

On the one hand, the ability to purchase items with a simple tap on a screen has made it easier for people to get what they want when they want it.

> *For example, if you're hungry and want a quick snack, you can order food through a delivery app and have it arrive at your door in just a few minutes.*

This convenience can be especially appealing for younger people who have grown up with technology and are used to instant access to information and goods.

However, this instant gratification, or the ability to have what you want right now, can be a dangerous trap. When you can buy something with a few clicks or a tap, it can be harder to control your spending. Additionally, the temptation to buy now and pay later can lead to overspending and debt. This is especially true when combined with targeted advertising and the influence of social media, which can create a constant urge to buy things you don't necessarily need.

It's important to be aware of instant gratification's potential risks and drawbacks of instant gratification and to practice good money management habits to avoid overspending and debt.

. . . .

FINTECH AND THE FUTURE OF PERSONAL FINANCE

Fintech, or financial technology, has a major impact on how we manage our money and the financial services industry. The latest advancements in fintech are making it easier for people to save, invest, and manage their money by offering new and innovative financial products and services. There are many examples of fintech products and services.

- **Mobile banking apps:** These apps allow you to access your bank account from your smartphone or tablet, making it easy to view your account balances, transfer money, and pay bills.

- **Digital wallets:** Digital wallets, such as Apple Pay and Google Pay, allow you to store your credit and debit card information securely in one place, making it easier to make payments with your phone.

- **Robo-advisors:** Robo-advisors are online investment management services that use algorithms to create and manage portfolios based on your financial goals and risk tolerance.

How to Avoid Overspending

Setting a budget and sticking to it
Having a clear idea of how much you can afford to spend each month can help you resist the urge to splurge on unnecessary purchases.

Waiting before making a purchase
Before making a purchase, take a step back and ask yourself if you really need the item. Try waiting 24 hours.

Unsubscribing from marketing emails
Marketing emails and advertisements can be tempting, but unsubscribing can help reduce the temptation to spend.

Turning off push notifications
Push notifications from shopping apps can be especially tempting. Consider turning off push notifications.

Deleting shopping apps altogether
Removing shopping apps on your mobile device helps reduce the temptation to scroll, tap & purchase.

Finding alternative ways to spend your time
Instead of shopping, find alternative activities that bring you joy, such as exercise, reading, or spending time with friends and family.

Using cash
Try to use cash instead of a debit or credit card. Using cash can make it easier to stick to a budget and help you avoid overspending.

- **P2P lending:** P2P lending platforms like LendingClub and Prosper allow you to lend money directly to individuals or small businesses, bypassing traditional banks.

- **Cryptocurrencies:** Cryptocurrencies like Bitcoin and Ethereum are digital currencies that use encryption techniques to secure transactions. While still relatively new and highly volatile, cryptocurrencies have the potential to change traditional finance by offering a decentralized and borderless alternative to traditional money.

These new products and services are not only making it easier for people to manage their money, but they are also providing more accessible and affordable financial services to people who may have been previously excluded from the traditional financial system. Overall, fintech is making it easier for people to take control of their finances and build wealth for the future.

FINANCE IN THE FUTURE

It's difficult to predict what the future of finance will look like, but there are a few trends that suggest the industry will continue to become increasingly digital and more focused on meeting the needs of consumers.

One trend is the rise of open banking, which will give consumers more control over their financial data and make it easier to compare and switch between financial products and services. This could result in a more competitive and innovative financial services industry, with new startups and established players offering more personalized and user-friendly products and services.

Another trend is the growth of financial wellness and budgeting tools, which use technology to help people better understand their spending habits and make informed financial decisions. This could lead to a future where people are more financially literate and in control of their money, reducing the need for financial intermediaries like banks.

Artificial intelligence and machine learning are also expected to play a bigger role in finance, helping to automate and streamline processes, reduce risk, and improve the customer experience. This could lead to the development of new financial products and services that are more accessible and affordable, especially for people who have traditionally been underserved by the financial system.

Overall, the future of finance is likely to be shaped by technology and the changing needs of consumers. The focus will be on making finance more accessible, affordable, and user-friendly, to empower people to take control of their financial futures.

It's going to be an exciting journey. Just as the iPhone changed how we interact with technology, it's possible fintech may change how we interact with money.

LET'S GET STARTED!!!

While money isn't everything, it does play a big role in our lives. Having the skills to manage it effectively can greatly impact our well-being and future success. By reading this book, you've taken an important step towards becoming financially literate and empowered to make informed decisions about your money.

Through the different chapters in this book, you've learned about the basics of money, from earning it to saving it and spending it wisely. You now know what a budget is, how interest works, and how to avoid scams. You understand credit scoring and why having a good score can help you in the future.

Congratulations on being empowered with the knowledge you need to be smart with your hard-earned money! Just like building a solid foundation is crucial for any structure to stand the test of time, reading this book has laid the foundation for your finances.

You've taken an important first step toward achieving long-term financial success. Now it's time to put what you have learned into practice. Start budgeting today, keep an eye out for great deals, save in advance for those big purchases, and protect yourself from online scams and frauds.

Most importantly, never stop learning, and don't be afraid to ask for help if you're unsure about something. Knowledge is power, but having the support of friends and family can be invaluable!

With the right attitude and determination, you'll soon have a healthy relationship with money and a secure financial future.

Good luck!

THANKS
FOR READING OUR
BOOK!

We hope it has been helpful in teaching your teen important financial skills that will serve them well throughout their life.

We would be so grateful if you could take a few seconds to leave an honest review or a star rating on Amazon. (A star rating takes just a couple of clicks).

By leaving a review, you'll be helping other parents discover this financial resource for their teens.

To leave a review & help spread the word

SCAN
HERE

JOIN OUR
ADVANCE READER
GROUP

and get FREE advance access to all our latest books!

To join our exclusive group:

SCAN
HERE